Write and Communicate Like a Professional

Write and Communicate Like a Professional

Kathryn Rosser Raign
Jake VanderVaate

University of North Texas Press
Denton, Texas

Printed in the United States of America.

10 9 8 7 6 5 4 3 2 1

Permissions:
University of North Texas Press
1155 Union Circle #311336
Denton, TX 76203-5017

The paper used in this book meets the minimum requirements of the American National Standard for Permanence of Paper for Printed Library Materials, z39.48.1984. Binding materials have been chosen for durability.

Library of Congress Cataloging-in-Publication Data

  Raign, Kathryn Rosser, author. | VanderVaate, Jake, author. | VanderVaate, Jake, author.
  Write and communicate like a professional / Kathryn Rosser Raign and Jake VanderVaate.
    pages cm
  Denton, Texas : University of North Texas Press, [2023]
  Includes bibliographical references and index.
  ISBN-13 978-1-57441-916-0 (paperback)
  1. LCSH: Technical writing—Handbooks, manuals, etc.
2. English language—Technical English—Handbooks, manuals, etc. 3. Communication of technical information—Handbooks, manuals, etc.

T11 .R34 2023
808.06/66–dc23/eng/20230501

                    2023017146

Typeset by vPrompt eServices.

Contents

Introduction

Everywhere we look, we see the written word: in books, in magazines, on the sides of buses, on the train, on Twitter, in emails, in texts. If we think about the sheer volume of words that we are expected to read each day, the task can seem overwhelming, but we can categorize all those words, which will help us prioritize our tasks.

In this book, we will focus on professional writing:

- What is it?
- How is it different from other types of writing?
- What exactly will I learn in this book?

These are important questions.

How Is Professional Writing Different from Other Types of Writing?

One of the best ways to understand what professional writing is by understanding what it's **not**.

Professional Writing Is Not Creative Writing

The many forms of creative writing—-memoirs, novels, short stories, poems, graphic novels, movie scripts—have several things in common. Their primary goal is not to provide the sort of information that will help a reader complete a task. Instead, a creative work is meant to have an emotional impact that allows the reader to share the writer's artistic vision. We read creative works for the simple pleasure of enjoying the writer's art. Creative writing does not have to justify its existence. Professional writing does.

Professional Writing Is Informational

You may think that it is the subject matter that determines whether a piece of writing is informational or creative, but it's not. We can write about the same topic both creatively and informatively. For example, let's say we are writing about cats. Here is a passage from *Alice's Adventures in Wonderland*:

[Alice] was a little startled by seeing the Cheshire Cat sitting on a bough of a tree a few yards off. The cat only grinned when it saw Alice. It looked good-natured, she thought: still it had very long claws and a great many teeth, so she felt it ought to be treated with respect.

"Cheshire Puss," she began, rather timidly, as she did not at all know whether it would like the name; however, it only grinned a little wider. "Come, it's pleased so far," thought Alice, and she went on. "Would you tell me, please, which way I ought to go from here?"

"That depends a great deal of where you want to get to," said the Cat.

"I don't much care where—" said Alice.

"Then it doesn't matter which way you go," said the Cat.

"—so long as I get somewhere," Alice added as explanation.

"Oh, you're sure to do that," said the Cat, "if you only walk long enough." (Carroll 1869, 89–90)

The subject matter of this passage is a request for directions from Alice to the Cat. However, as Alice and the Cat are both fictional characters, and cats do not talk, we know this is from a fictional story. Now let's look at another way of writing about cats:

Dear Tenant,

One of your neighbors told me that they saw a cat sitting in your apartment window. While Green Acres apartment complex is pet-friendly, those tenants who keep pets must pay a pet deposit. According to my records, yours has not been paid. If you intend to keep the cat, please bring me a one-time payment of $250, and expect your rent to increase by $15 a month. You must make your payment by the last day of the month.

If you have any questions or concerns, feel free to call me or drop by the office.

Sincerely,

Mary Larry 111-111-1111

This message was sent from an apartment manager to a tenant via email. Clearly, the message is not fictional. The sender is addressing a real-world problem that requires a real solution. This is an example of professional writing.

Now that you know what professional communication is, let's talk about its purpose.

What Are Some Examples of Professional Writing?

Professional writing is typically divided into three categories:

Instructional

To tell someone how to do something

- Employee handbooks
- Videos
- Infographics
- Memos outlining new office procedures

Informational

To provide information about a specific subject

- Reports
- Financial statements
- Meeting minutes
- A memo outlining changes in management

Persuasive

To persuade someone to take a desired action

- Proposals
- Press Releases
- Advertisements
- Memos requesting your cooperation

Examples of types of professional writing that can occur in any of these categories include

- Letters
- Emails
- Texts
- Memos
- Handbooks
- Reports
- Agendas
- Press releases
- Newsletters

While all of these are important forms of professional communication, we will be focusing on those written forms of professional communication you will use most often:

- Emails
- Memos
- Short reports

However, the principles you will learn are applicable to all type of professional communication, and in the next course,

2700—Advanced Professional Communication, we will practice writing longer documents: instructions, proposals, formal reports, and job materials.

Why Do You Need to Know How to Write Professionally?

According to an article published in *Inc.*,

> Businesses are spending billions each year on remedial writing training, and in a modern workplace that requires employees to spend hours each day sending emails, writing reports, and interacting with clients, weak writing skills can be a major hindrance to business growth (not to mention the damage poor writing skills can do to public perception of a business's brand.)
>
> According to the National Association of Colleges and Employers, 73.4% of employers want a candidate with strong written communication skills. Written communication was the number three most desired quality overall, behind leadership skills and ability to work as a team member.
>
> While much of the modern educational system puts a focus on STEM education (that's science, technology, engineering, and mathematics), it seems that now, more than ever, it's writing that is becoming the sought-after skill in the hiring market. (Moore 2016)

TIP	**73.4 percent** of employers value employees with strong written communication skills

You might have chosen this book because you had to, but we hope these statistics have proven how essential writing is to your professional success. It's easy for everyone to list "good communication skills," on their resume without providing any proof, but after reading this book, you will have documented evidence of your skills as a writer! We have written this text so that you can easily find information.

Look for these study aids:

TIP	This is for tips that can add to comprehension of the subject matter.
NOTE	Every time you see this icon, you'll know we are providing you with an example of a concept we've been discussing. Examples like this help your brain hardwire the concepts.
IMPORTANT	When you see this icon, you'll know we're providing a clue for success.
CAUTION	Grammar gremlins are everywhere, so look to this icon for quick explanations about annoying grammar gripes and how to solve them.

Each module includes four sections:

Learn
In this section, we provide the information you need to complete the rest of the sections in the module.

Assess
You won't know if you've learned what you've read until you test yourself. Each chapter has a quiz that will let you do this.

Engage
The best way to learn is by sharing your ideas with others. These discussion activities let you practice the skills being taught in the module and get feedback from your classmates.

Apply
The best way to learn to write is by writing. Each module includes a writing task that we will evaluate so you can get constructive criticism.

Let's get started!

Audience

Learning Objectives

- Use your understanding of your audience to make effective writing choices.
- Apply the rhetorical situation to answer questions as you write.
- Understand the difference between writer-based and reader-based writing.
- Understand how to be a reader-based writer.

Learn—Audience

When we write, our audience should be our most important concern.

Audience Analysis

Our communication always has an audience. Sometimes we might be communicating primarily with ourselves, and other times we might communicate with one, ten, twenty, or a thousand people. To communicate effectively with everyone, we need to understand that there are two types of writing:

- Writer based
- Reader based

Each of these has purposes, but it is important to know the difference between the two.

Writer-Based Writing

When we write **only** for ourselves, we are engaging in writer-based writing. We call it writer based because our only audience is ourselves, so we don't have to worry about whether anyone will understand what we write. Here are some examples of writer-based writing:

- A journal
- A grocery list
- Notes from a meeting or class
- A Post-it note reminding you to do something

When we do this type of writing, we can use our own personal shorthand, leave out details, and take shortcuts because *we* know what we mean. However, when we think "writer based" when we are writing for an audience other than ourselves, our communication is likely to be ineffective. For example, if you asked a colleague to summarize a meeting that you couldn't attend, and they sent you this email, would you have a clear understanding of what occurred during the meeting and how it applies to you?

- Met with M.
- Discussed proj.
- Remember to send her numbers ASAP.
- Assigned jobs.
- All agreed.

Clearly, your colleague wasn't thinking of you as they wrote.

- What project was discussed?
- Who is M?
- Are you supposed to send M numbers?
- If so, what numbers, and when?
- What job were you assigned?

The message makes complete sense to the writer because the writer attended the meeting. Because you didn't, your colleague **should** have been thinking "reader based."

Reader-Based Writing

Reader-based writing puts the reader, **not** the writer, first. This textbook is an example of reader-based writing, though our notes as we wrote were writer based. When you think "reader based" you ask yourself:

- What does my reader already know?
- What doesn't my reader know?
- What information does my reader need?
- How can I most effectively share that information with my reader?
- How will my reader feel about my message? Good or bad?

When you work from this mindset, you'll communicate more effectively because you will be putting your readers' needs first. Of course, this type of writing takes more time and is more difficult; that's why we wrote this book. We want to help you become a reader-based communicator!

Become a Reader-Based Communicator

To become a reader-based communicator, you need to engage in reader-based thinking. To do this, you must get in the habit of thinking before communicating. Specifically, you need to think about your audience, purpose, and reason for communicating. These three categories are what make up the rhetorical situation. The rhetorical situation is the key to all communication.

Let's look at an example.

You work for a large industrial bread factory. Your company has just purchased new industrial mixers to be used on the factory floor. You were asked to write instructions for using these new mixers. These instructions are crucial for several reasons:

- To prevent injuries to the employees
- To prevent damage to the machines
- To lower employees' stress
- To increase productivity

Which of the following choices do you think would be best?

a. A poster on the wall above the coffeemaker in the break room
b. A one-page paper printout that is placed in each employee's mailbox
c. A one-page paper printout left next to each mixer
d. A one-page laminated set of instructions permanently attached to the work surface next to the mixer

If you chose **d**, you are correct. And our use of the rhetorical situation is what will make that clear.

Audience

Based on what we know, we can make these educated guesses:

- While the employees were very comfortable with the old mixers, which share some similarities with the new ones, they are still feeling some stress and anxiety as they learn how to use the new ones.
- The fact that the factory floor is loud, messy, and chaotic makes it more difficult for the employees to focus on instructions.
- The employees need to be able to consult the instructions quickly without leaving their mixers.
- Mixers are used to mix eggs, oil, flour, sugar, and other wet and sticky ingredients. The employees' hands might also get messy.

Purpose

Both the employees and the management of the company have a similar purpose, so how can the document itself help achieve that purpose?

- In order to allow employees to consult the instructions without leaving their mixers, the instructions should be permanently affixed to the workstation. This will prevent the instructions from being lost or misplaced.

- Because the instructions are exposed to wet and sticky substances, they should be laminated. A piece of unprotected paper cannot be cleaned and would quickly become illegible.
- Because the employees' hands will be occupied when they consult the instructions, all the information must be on the front of the page.

Reason

To ensure that the reason for writing the instructions is met, the writers should consider all of the discoveries we made previously. At this point, you might be thinking, "Sure, that kind of analysis is easy for you, but what about me?" No worries. Let's talk about some strategies for analyzing your audience.

Consider Your Audience

Every audience is made up of real people with real needs, questions, and purposes. Your job as a reader-based communicator is to analyze your audience so you can anticipate how to meet their needs, answer their questions, and help them achieve their purpose. To do this, you need to step inside your readers' shoes and view the world from their perspective. Once you've done that, you can begin answering your questions.

What Does the Audience Need?

What do your readers need from your communication?

- Information?
- Answers?
- Instructions?
- An overview?
- A confirmation?

Until you determine what your readers need, you can't decide what to include in your communication. You can take this a step further by asking these questions:

- What do they already know?
- What don't they know?

What Does the Audience Already Know?

To answer this question, you need to think about what information your readers have had access to:

- Did they attend the meeting?
- Did they read the report?
- Were they copied on the email?
- Are they a member of the team?

Answering these questions will help you avoid telling your readers what they already know.

What Doesn't the Audience Know?

Again, you need to ask the same questions, but this time, you are looking for gaps in their knowledge. For example, if your reader didn't get to read the original report, you might need to provide an overview of that report to help them fill in the gaps in your readers' knowledge. Make sense?

Once you have determined what you need to include in your communication and what you don't, you need to consider the best form of communication.

What's the Most Effective Form of Communication?

When we communicate, we have lots of options for how to communicate:

- Text message
- Instant message (IM)
- Audio call
- Email
- Informal report
- Formal report
- Presentation
- Conversation

Each of these have uses.

Form	Use
Text message	To send a text message, you must have someone's phone number. So you will only send texts to people you know well. Texts are also short, so you wouldn't use them for complicated or important messages.
IM	If your company's system supports instant messaging, you can use it—but again, only if you have a short message to send.
Call	Sometimes it's best to hear someone's voice. In those cases, a call is best, but only call people with whom you work closely. For example, never call your supervisor unless they ask you to. Phone messages work best for quick questions or confirmations: Want to grab lunch? Can you take notes during the meeting?
Informal report	Informal reports are short—one to five pages—and normally use a memo format. You can send them electronically, attach them to an email, or print and distribute them. Informal reports are best for providing more complex information that must be explained in detail. A new company policy would probably be communicated as an informal report and distributed by email, or perhaps on the company website.
Formal report	Formal reports are longer and include title pages, abstracts, and a table of contents. They often use color and are frequently printed for distribution. An example of a formal report would be a quarterly earnings report.
Presentation	Presentations give you the opportunity to connect with a larger audience on a more personal level. Presentations are a good way to get people excited about something. Companies like Apple and Google use presentations to introduce new products.
Conversation	Sometimes it's important to keep a communication confidential. A conversation is the best way to do that. Even though the participants can tell others about the conversation, there is no written record. A good time to have a conversation would be to discuss a personnel issue.

Every time we communicate, we have a purpose for communicating, and the receiver has a purpose for listening or reading.

Purpose

We choose to engage with some forms of communication because it's enjoyable: films, theater, websites, podcasts, and fiction.

But very few of us read reports or instructions for enjoyment. We read them for a purpose:

- To learn something
- To make a decision
- To complete a task
- To make a request
- To solve a problem

For example, when I look up instructions on how to create a pivot table in Excel, I am reading those instructions for a specific purpose: to create a pivot table.

We also communicate for specific purposes, and our purpose helps us decide how to communicate effectively:

- To instruct we use a numbered list of steps
- To inform we provide specific information
- To persuade we make an argument

If you don't know **why** you are communicating with someone, how can you know **how** to communicate?

Reason

In addition to understanding who we are communicating with and why, we also need to think about what reason prompted us to communicate in the first place:

- I haven't received my tax refund. I need to email my accountant and ask why.
- My supervisor asked me to provide them with a summary of the meeting I attended. I need to write an informal report and attach it to an email.
- My team doesn't know how to schedule meetings in Microsoft Teams. I need to write instructions and send them to everyone.

Another important aspect of considering your audience is remembering that we are all different.

Practice Inclusive Writing

It's easy to make the mistake of assuming that the people to whom you are writing are just like you. Of course they love football, cats, and homemade pizza. They know you're a good person, so they won't get their feelings hurt if you don't waste time asking how they are, and who doesn't like a good joke?

But this attitude is more than writer based; it's just plain self-centered. Thanks to technology, we can communicate with anyone, anywhere, anytime. So we have to be even more mindful of what we say and how we say it. Here are some important tips to remember.

Avoid Non-Inclusive References

When you use an expression like "let's table that issue," "the cat's out of the bag," or "piece of cake," you are likely to confuse anyone who is not from the United States. And even within the States, expressions like "I'm fixing to write the report" can be confusing to someone who didn't grow up in the south. The best way to avoid this problem is by avoiding these types of colloquial references. Use plain language:

- Let's put that issue on hold.
- Everyone knows now.
- It's easy.
- I'm about to write the report.

Understand the Other Person's Communication Culture

This attitude also applies to how we assign gender. Everyone has the right to decide how they identify, though some people may choose not to share this information. If someone does share a preference (i.e., I use the pronouns she/her), then honor it. Never assume that specific professions are tied to a specific gender. Anyone can be a teacher, doctor, nurse, baker, etc.

Don't make assumptions (they really can make an "ass" out of "u" and "me") based on your personal observations. How someone looks does not logically determine what language(s) they speak, what place they call home, or what personal beliefs they might hold.

When writing to someone you know is from a different culture, you can increase your chances of a positive outcome by considering whether they come from a high- or low-context communication culture.

Low- Versus High-Context Cultures

Some cultures favor high-context communication and some favor low-context communication. The United States is a low-context culture; we prefer direct, simple communication. In other words, we don't waste words on niceties or small talk. High-context countries, like Mexico or India, prefer indirect, subtle, less explicit communication:

- Low context: Your report is due by 5:00 pm today.
- High context: It is very important for you to finish your report as soon as possible.

If you don't understand whether the person you are communicating with is from a high- or low-context culture, you are likely to misunderstand each other.

Figure 1.1 International flags.

Avoid Communication Roadblocks

No matter how careful we are when we write, it's easy for our good intentions to go sideways, so avoid these roadblocks.

Not Providing Context

Context is critical when communicating with others. Inadequate context often leads to further back-and-forth communication between all parties because the original message didn't have clear intent.

When communicating with others, especially in an increasingly asynchronous workplace, consider adding the following items to your message:

- Who
- What
- When
- Where
- Why
- How

Adding any or all of these pieces of information can provide context that helps your audience understand your message.

Consider this example:

A low-context conversation

Anna	Hey, have you had the chance to work on that report you said you'd send me?
Bob	Hello, I worked with Peter this morning.

Bob's message is subject to multiple interpretations.

- What did Bob work on with Peter?
- Is what Bob and Peter worked on relevant to Anna's request?
  Consider these modifications:

The same conversation with more added context

Anna	Hey, have you had the chance to work on that report you said you'd send me?
Bob	Hello. No, but I worked on a similar report with Peter this morning. I'll send you that report, which should answer most of your questions about your report. Let me know if you have any questions after consulting that report.

This version offers more information and context about Anna's request.

CAUTION	**Smash that send button and ask questions later?** Ask any writer what step they skip when they're in a hurry, and they will probably answer (if they're honest) proofreading. After all, it was just a two-sentence email, what can go wrong? • Shift leader can become sh&* leader • AM can become PM
CAPITALIZATION	Do you ever wonder why we capitalize some words and not others? Here are the basic rules: • Capitalize proper nouns: a person's name, the name of a place, the name of a product, etc. • Capitalize titles when they are followed by a name: President Biden, CEO Steven Jobs, Colonel Rosser, the president, the dean • Capitalize college majors when they are languages: Spanish, engineering, computer science, Greek • For headings, capitalize every word that is not a preposition, article, or coordinating conjunction

If You Don't Know, Ask

Sometimes asking questions is a daunting prospect because we attach all kinds of baggage to the process of asking:

- I'll look stupid
- I'll look like I wasn't paying attention in the meeting
- I'll annoy the person I'm asking
- It will take too long
- I have a pretty good idea what the answer is, so why bother?

Don't write until you are fully informed about the audience, purpose and occasion surrounding the topic you are writing about.

Assess—Audience

1. What is writer-based writing?
   a. Writing intended to be read only by ourselves
   b. Writing intended to be read mainly by others
   c. All writing

2. What is reader-based writing?
   a. Writing intended to be read mainly by others
   b. Writing intended to be read only by ourselves
   c. All writing

3. When you write for yourself, it doesn't matter if others can clearly understand it; however, when you write for others, the only thing that matters is if they can clearly understand it.
   a. True
   b. False

4. What are the main things to consider when writing for your readers?
   a. How to meet your readers' needs, answer their questions, and help them achieve their purpose
   b. What you know about the topic, how to write the information so that you understand it, and how to help your readers understand it

    c. How to physically present the information so that your readers will have it when they need it and how to make it look like a professional publishing company made the document

5. What do you need to consider about your readers? Select all that apply.
   a. Their needs
   b. Their knowledge
   c. Their culture
   d. The purpose and occasion for writing to them

6. Using slang expressions is a great way to clearly convey your meaning to your readers, especially to readers of other cultures.
   a. True
   b. False

7. What is the difference between communication in high-context and low-context cultures?
   a. Communication in low-context cultures gets straight to the point and states the message in no uncertain terms. Communication in high-context cultures includes formalities and the "real" message is somewhat implied rather than clearly stated.
   b. Communication in low-context cultures is buried in niceties and formalities. Communication in high-context cultures gets straight to the point.
   c. Communication in low-context cultures doesn't consider the feelings of the receiver of the message. Communication in high-context cultures does, even at the risk of obscuring the message.

8. Assume you're working on a project with a partner. You finished your part and are waiting for them to send you their portion of the work. This is the first time you've worked together, but you know your partner is from a different culture and is used to high-context communication. How could you politely ask them to send you their work?

a. In an email with a message like "I hope work on your piece of the project has been going well. I've got my portion done. Let me know when you're ready and we can combine our pieces. I hope Wednesday won't be too soon?"

b. In an email with a message like "I'm done with my part. When will your portion be ready? We need to start merging them by Wednesday."

c. In a text with a message like "Ya done on the project, fam?"

9. The only problem created by not proofreading is making yourself look unprofessional; typos couldn't possibly affect the meaning of your message.

a. True

b. False

10. You should never send an email when you're angry.

a. True

b. False

Engage—Audience

In this module, we've been talking about the importance of audience. For this discussion you are going to respond to this scenario:

Scenario One

Your supervisor has grown increasingly frustrated by the amount of coffee being consumed by the team. In the past, you've used an honor system to pay for coffee and supplies like creamer, sugar, and cups, but contributions have stopped coming in even though coffee consumption is up. Your supervisor is tired of paying for this expense out of his pocket, so he wrote the following memo. Because he respects your skills as a writer, he asked you to look at it before he sends it:

Memo

Date: April 3, 2022
To: All of you coffee guzzlers
From: John
Re: Out of Control Coffee Consumption

When I bought the coffeemaker for the team last year, we all agreed that everyone would make REGULAR donations to the jar sitting next to it. You know, the jar labeled COFFEE CONTRIBUTIONS!

Guess what? NO ONE is contributing except me! I can't afford to keep paying for your coffee addictions. Either you all start paying, or you can stop drinking.

Sorry tea drinkers. You can ignore this memo. While I don't get why you drink weak brown dishwater, I do appreciate that you don't cost me any money.

Your Task

For this discussion, you will write a memo to John offering constructive criticism. Before you write your memo, complete the following steps:

1. Identify three specific examples within the memo that demonstrate that the writer wasn't considering his audience as he wrote.
2. Locate examples from your readings to support your criticism.
3. Include specific examples from the memo to support your suggestions.
4. Follow best practices when writing your memo.

Apply—Audience

In this module, we've been talking about the importance of audience. In our discussion, you had the chance to practice writing a memo in response to someone else's writing. For this assignment, you will do the same thing, so remember to apply the feedback I gave you. You are going to respond to this scenario.

Scenario Two

No one has enjoyed COVID, but over the past eighteen months, the eight members of your team have enjoyed the freedom of working from home. Everyone agrees that not having to commute to the office saves them time, which makes them more productive. They also like the money they save on gas. Several people also feel like their opportunity to eat a healthy meal at lunchtime, followed by a short walk, has improved their health. You agree with your team and would be happy continuing to work from home. Unfortunately, your department supervisor feels differently. She is planning to have each of the three teams in her department begin working from the office in two weeks. Because you are the leader of the writing team, she asked you to read her memo before she sends it out to everyone:

Supervisor Memo Example

Date: April 3, 2022
To: Time to Put Those Sweats and Slippers Away
From: Jane
Re: Off the couch and back to the desk

I know you've all enjoyed sleeping in and taking long lunches, but it's time to get back to the real world.

On June 3, two months from today, I expect everyone to be back at their desk and ready to work hard. It's been fun having a break so you could play with your kids and your dogs, but you need to buckle down and do the jobs you get paid for. Productivity has to get back to normal. Two weeks should be plenty of time to make whatever arrangements you need to make, so no excuses from anyone. If I can do it, so can you! We are in this together!

Your Task

For this assignment, you will write a memo to Jane offering constructive criticism. Before you write your memo, complete the following steps:

1. Identify three specific examples within the memo that demonstrate that the writer wasn't considering her audience as she wrote.
2. Locate examples from your class readings to support your criticism.
3. Include specific examples from the memo to support your suggestions.
4. Follow best practices when writing your memo.

Assignment Rubric

	Superior	*Above Average*	*Average*	*Below Average*	*Failing*
Content	20 points	15 points	10 points	5 points	0 points
	Includes all of the required elements of the assignment.	Includes all of the required elements, though some are underdeveloped.	Includes most of the required elements.	Includes some of the required elements.	Does not include all of the required elements.
Style	20 points	15 points	10 points	5 points	0 points
	The writing is clear and concise and avoids unnecessary use of passive constructions.	The writing is clear and concise and generally avoids unnecessary use of passive constructions.	The writing is mostly clear and concise and mostly avoids unnecessary use of passive constructions.	The writing is occasionally clear and concise but does not avoid unnecessary use of passive constructions.	The style is inappropriate or unclear.

	Superior	*Above Average*	*Average*	*Below Average*	*Failing*
Design	20 points	15 points	10 points	5 points	0 points
	The document has a clear visual hierarchy and the writer uses appropriate methods of presentation such as lists and tables.	The document has a clear visual hierarchy and the writer uses some appropriate methods of presentation such as lists and tables.	The document has a basic visual hierarchy and the writer occasionally uses appropriate methods of presentation such as lists and tables.	The document's visual hierarchy is weak and the writer doesn't use appropriate methods of presentation such as lists and tables.	The document has no visual hierarchy.
Structure	20 points	15 points	10 points	5 points	0 points
	The organization of the document is clear and logical and makes strong use of topic sentences and transitions.	The organization of the document is generally clear and logical and makes some use of topic sentences and transitions.	The document has organization and occasionally uses topic sentences and transitions.	The structure is weak and the writer rarely uses topic sentences or transitions.	The document has no structure.
Correctness	20 points	15 points	10 points	5 points	0 points
	The document has no errors.	The document has 2–3 errors.	The document has 4–5 errors.	The document has 6–7 errors.	The document has 8 or more errors.

Correctness

Learning objectives

- Recognize the parts of speech.
- Distinguish phrases from clauses.
- Recognize the four types of sentences.
- Understand how to punctuate the four types of sentences.
- Use apostrophes and colons correctly.

Learn—Correctness

One of the best ways to ensure that others consider you a professional is to write like a professional, and professional writers don't
make careless mistakes. Consider this: If you attended a presentation,
would you take the information you received seriously if the speaker
showed up wearing ratty jeans, flip-flops, and a stained T-shirt?

Figure 2.1 Casual wear isn't good for professional presentations.

What if the speaker passed out handouts that they'd hand-written in purple pen with words crossed out and replaced?

Fair or not, impressions matter, and when you are not physically present, your writing represents you. If your writing includes errors, you are damaging your credibility and increasing the likelihood that your readers will assume

- You don't know any better
- You're too lazy to proofread
- You don't care
- You can't be trusted to do a good job

If this is how your colleagues assess your abilities, your career is in serious danger.

I understand that learning about grammar and punctuation might not be your idea of fun. Honestly, I don't love exercising, but I exercise because I know the benefits outweigh the negatives (pain, sweat, etc.). The same is true when it comes to learning how to write correctly. Besides, you must know it's important, or you wouldn't have chosen this book! Grammar and punctuation are big topics, and we could devote hundreds of pages to them. But our goal isn't to cover everything.

Our goal is to give you the big pictures so that you can avoid making the most common errors. If you want more detail, you can buy the *Chicago Manual of Style*.

We'll cover these topics in this module:

- Parts of speech
- Clauses
- Phrases
- Sentence types
- Agreement
- Quotation marks, colons, and apostrophes

If we break something complicated into pieces, we can understand it more easily, so we're going to start by looking at the basic building blocks of any sentence—the parts of speech, the clause, and the phrase.

Parts of Speech

Before you can understand either grammar or punctuation, you have to understand the basic pieces of a sentence.

We use nouns, pronouns, verbs, adverbs, adjectives, prepositions, conjunctions, and interjections:

Part of Speech	Definition	Example
Noun	person, place, or thing	woman, house, Australia
Pronoun	a word used in place of a noun	he, his, they, it
Verb	a word that expresses action	run, walk, seem, is, write
Adverb	a word that describes anything other than a noun	quickly, cautiously, well
Adjective	a word that describes a noun	old, broken, intelligent
Article	a word placed before a noun or pronoun to form a phrase	a, an, the
Prepositions	words that identify time or position	before, until, with, under
Conjunctions	words that combine a series of words, phrases, or clauses	and, but, however
Interjections	words used to express strong emotions	ouch!, wow!, darn!

You will combine the parts of speech to form clauses and phrases.

Clauses

There are two types of clauses:

- Independent (a complete sentence): I ate dinner.
- Dependent (not a complete sentence): although I ate dinner.

A sentence must have at least one independent clause, but it does not have to have a dependent clause.

Independent clauses must have both a noun and a verb.

- The noun acts as the **subject** of the sentence—who or what is doing the action of the verb.
- The verb and any adverbs or adjectives make up the **predicate**.

Independent clauses can also be called simple sentences:

independent clause = simple sentence

Every sentence must have a subject.

Subjects

The bones of a sentence are its subject. The subject is either who or what is doing the action of the sentence's verb, or what the sentence is about:

The subject is bolded in the following examples

> **The dog** chased me down the street.
>
> **Nancy** left the party.
>
> **The meeting** was canceled.

In the first sentence, the dog performs the action, and in the second sentence, Nancy does. In the last sentence, the meeting tells us what the sentence is about.

The subject is like the bones of a body because it supports everything happening in the sentence. Subjects come in different forms, but usually subjects are one of these:

Nouns

A person, place, or thing (e.g., Michael, the woman, the experiment)

> **Michael** completed the experiment.

Gerunds

A participial verb (a verb that ends in **ing**) being used as a noun (e.g., smoking, running, eating)

> **Running** strengthens your heart.

Pronouns

A noun that renames someone or something (e.g., he, she, it, they, we, us, there)

> **She** runs five miles every day.

Relative pronouns

A pronoun that begins a relative clause (a type of dependent clause) (e.g., who, whom, which, that)

> I know someone **who** runs ten miles a day.

Below are more examples of different subjects.

Examples of parts of speech

Part of Speech	Definition	Example	In Action
Noun	A person, place, or thing	Michael, the report, the supervisor	The CFO approved the budget.
Gerund	A participial verb (a verb that ends in "ing") used as a noun	Smoking, running, managing	Managing monthly expenditures is part of the job.
Pronoun	A noun that renames something	He, she, it, they, we, us, this, these	He accepted the position.
Relative Pronouns	A pronoun that begins with a relative clause	Who, whom, which, that	My supervisor, who has worked here five years, just received a promotion.

Subjects don't work alone. They need verbs to make things happen.

Verbs

The portion of the sentence that contains the verb is called the predicate. The predicate is everything that comes after the subject.

Predicates in action

Subject	Predicate
I	submitted the proposal to Gary.
George	sold his father's clothes to the thrift shop.
Bob	wants a new car for Christmas.

The predicate always contains a verb and may also contain a direct object, possibly an indirect object, or a subject complement. Nouns always act as objects and complements. The verb will determine which of these it contains. The muscle of a clause is the verb—the word or words that provide the action.

> I (subject) submitted (verb) the proposal (direct object) to Gary (indirect object).

There are four types of verbs:

- Transitive
- Intransitive
- Linking
- To be

Transitive Verbs
A transitive verb always takes a direct object. The direct object tells us to whom or what the action was done.

Direct Objects
A transitive verb needs a direct object to complete its meaning. This is because a transitive verb indicates an action that must be done to someone or something. For example, you can't just "throw" you must throw something. The something you throw is the direct object of the verb:

> She threw a **fit**.
>
> My father bought a new **car**.
>
> He lifted the heavy **load**.

In each case, the subject of the sentence does the action (threw, bought, lifted) to something (fit, car, load).

Indirect Objects

A direct object may be followed by an indirect object—a noun or pronoun that tells to whom or for whom the action of the sentence is being done. For example, if you throw a ball, you normally throw it to someone. If you serve dinner, you serve it to someone.

Look at these examples:

> John threw the ball (direct object) to the boy (indirect object).
>
> The wait person served dinner (direct object) to her guests (indirect object).
>
> I told my secret (direct object) to him (indirect object).

Indirect objects can also come before direct objects:

> John threw the boy (indirect object) his ball (direct object).
>
> The waiter served her guests (indirect object) dinner (direct object).
>
> I told him (indirect object) my secret (direct object).

As you can see, indirect objects can come before or after the direct object. Unlike transitive verbs, intransitive verbs do not need an object to complete their meaning.

Intransitive Verbs

An intransitive verb makes sense all by itself and doesn't require an object to take its action. For example, you have to throw something, but you don't have to sleep something. You just sleep. Look at these examples:

> The goldfish died.
>
> The movie ended.
>
> I slept.

Although intransitive verbs don't have objects, they can have adverbs that describe how the action was done:

> The goldfish died **suddenly**.
>
> The movie ended **early**.
>
> I slept **badly**.

Linking

A linking verb links the subject and subject complement. The subject complement describes or identifies the subject. The linking verbs include:

- look
- become
- stay
- seem
- grow
- prove
- smell
- appear
- remain
- feel
- sound

Linking verbs are always followed by a subject complement. The subject complement describes or renames the subject:

> The cat looks **sick**.
>
> The tree grew **tall**.
>
> The chemicals smell **terrible**.

To Be Verbs

To be verbs include all forms of the verb "to be":

- to be
- am

- was
- being
- is
- were
- been
- are
- have been

Like linking verbs, to-be verbs are followed by a subject complement:

> The house is a **mansion**.
>
> Last night, I was **tired**.
>
> Our experiment is a **lost cause**.

While every clause must have a subject and a verb, not every clause is independent. In fact, there are three types of clauses:

- Independent
- Dependent
- Relative

Understanding the difference between these three is crucial to your understanding of what a sentence is and how to punctuate it.

Types of Clauses

You already know that a clause has a subject and a predicate—which should mean that all clauses can stand alone. However, some clauses have been weakened by the addition of a word called a "subordinating conjunction."

Subordinating conjunctions make clauses so weak they must depend on another clause to complete their meaning and support them. These weak clauses are called "dependent" clauses because they cannot stand alone and must be supported by an independent clause. Clauses that begin with relative pronouns are called relative clauses. They cannot stand alone either unless they are questions. Let's look at each type of clause:

Independent Clauses

An independent clause is a simple sentence that can stand alone. It has both a subject and a verb, and depending on the type of verb, either a direct object, indirect object, subject complement, or phrase:

> I like to listen (transitive verb) to music (direct object).
>
> Sara is (to-be verb) my best friend (subject complement).
>
> I adopted (transitive verb) a new puppy (direct object).
>
> I slept (intransitive) on the sofa (prepositional phrase).

While an independent clause can stand alone, a dependent clause must be combined with an independent clause because the independent clause completes its meaning.

Dependent Clauses

When you add a subordinating conjunction to an independent clause, you make it dependent. The following is a list of commonly used subordinating conjunctions:

- after
- because
- in order that
- than
- when
- although
- before
- now that
- that
- whenever
- though
- where
- as if
- even

- though
- rather than
- till
- whereas
- as long as
- if
- since
- unless
- wherever
- as though
- if only
- so that
- until
- while

Placing any of these words at the beginning of an independent clause will make it dependent.

> I like to listen to music **because it relaxes me**.
>
> **Although I haven't known Sara long**, she is my best friend.
>
> My dog is very fat **because he eats the cat's food**.

In each of the examples above, we combined a dependent clause that would not make sense alone, with an independent clause that completed its meaning.

> **TIP**
>
> We'll talk about this more later, but notice that you only put a comma AFTER a dependent clause when it comes BEFORE the independent clause.

Relative Clauses
Relative clauses are also dependent, but in this case, they are dependent because they begin with a relative pronoun:

- which
- what
- who
- whom
- that
- whatever
- whose
- whoever
- whomever

Like a dependent clause, a relative clause must combine with an independent clause that finishes its meaning, **unless** it is used as a question:

> I like to listen to music (independent clause) **that is slow** (relative clause) because it relaxes me (dependent clause).

> Although I haven't known her long, Sara, **who lives next door** (relative clause in middle of dependent clause), is my best friend.
>
> My dog is very fat because he eats the cat's food, **which makes the cat angry** (relative clause).

Relative clauses can be independent when they are questions:

> Who called?

You can't have a sentence without a clause. Phrases, on the other hand, are optional rather than required.

Phrases

Phrases aren't essential, but they add detail and interest. They add style.

A phrase is a string of two or more words, but it can't stand alone as a sentence because it doesn't have both a subject and a verb; it has one or the other but not both. Consequently, phrases can provide extra information about the subject or verbs of an independent clause, and they can act as the object or complement of the subject. However, phrases cannot stand alone:

> **Until last night**, I slept in a warm bed.

In this example, the phrase "until last night" tells us when the action of the independent clause "I slept in a warm bed" occurred.

> **For the next seven days**, I will sleep **on the hard ground**.

In this example, we have two phrases. The first, "for the next seven days," tells us when the action occurs, and the second phrase, "on the hard ground," tells us where.

> Tina's **big brown** eyes quickly scanned the page of text **in front of her**.

In this sentence, the phrase "big brown" describes Tina's eyes, while the phrase "in front of her" tells us where the text is.

> I enjoy **long evening walks**.

In this last example, the phrase "long evening walks" acts as the direct object of enjoy.

Phrases come in many types, but they all have one thing in common; they have either a subject OR a verb, not both:

Prepositional phrases
Begin with prepositions: under the bridge, over the rainbow, into the wild

> I saved the proposal **on my computer**

Verbal phrases
Begin with some form of a verb: running the meeting, to wander the world, determined to win

> I stopped her **leaving the meeting**.

Gerund phrases

Like gerunds, always act as nouns: smoking paraphernalia, swimming gear

> Don't go to the beach without **swimming gear**.

Noun phrases

Can work as adjectives and describe other nouns, or they can be subject complements or objects:

> I don't know why she adopted the **big ugly cat** (direct object).
>
> John Banks, **the new CFO** (adjective), has twenty years of experience.
>
> The new project is **one big challenge** (subject complement).

Now that you understand the building blocks of a sentence, let's talk about the different types of sentences. But first, let's look at one of those reviews we promised.

Review

You can find all the review answers in the appendix at the end of the book.

Review 1

Identify each of the following as either a phrase, an independent clause, or a dependent clause.

1. Presenting the report
2. The engineers wrote it
3. Although they collaborated with the chemists
4. Late last night
5. From the board of directors

Review 2

Identify each clause (in bold) as dependent, independent, or relative.

1. **Although I worked all night**, I still didn't finish my report.
2. I didn't finish **because I lost my power**, and I hadn't saved my file.
3. **I should know better** since I've been working as a technical communicator for five years.
4. I had to start from scratch, **which was very frustrating**.
5. Since I've never missed a deadline before, **my team leader gave me an extension**.

Review 3

For each sentence, identify the subject; identify the verb; determine if the verb is transitive, intransitive, linking, or to be; and determine if the verb has a direct object, indirect object, or subject complement.

1. For many people, working from home is a new experience.
2. It was for me.
3. At first, I felt unmotivated, but I learned to stick to a schedule.
4. I have become very productive, and I can do more in less time because I have no distractions.
5. I will continue to work from home after the quarantine is lifted.

Sentence Types

Now that you are familiar with the pieces that make up a sentence, you can begin combining those pieces to make the four types of sentences:

- Simple
- Compound
- Complex
- Compound complex

To make it easier, we will use these abbreviations:

Term	Abbreviation
Independent clause	IC
Dependent clause	DC
Coordinating conjunction	CC
Subordinating conjunction	SC
Conjunctive adverb	CA
Correlative conjunction	COC
Phrase	P
Comma	C
Semicolon	Semi

We suggest you print out this list of abbreviations and keep it by your computer for quick reference.

Simple Sentences

A simple sentence is one independent clause and possibly one or more phrases. A phrase can come at the beginning of the sentence, at the end of the sentence, or in the middle of the sentence. A simple sentence never has more than one independent clause and never has a dependent clause.

> Simple sentence: one independent clause and one or more phrases

Look at these examples. Each sentence is followed by its formula:

> Historical (adjective) events (subject) are (to-be verb) often (adverb) made (subject complement) into movies (prepositional phrase). IC + P

> **NOTE**   At the end of this chapter, we'll provide a list of all the formulas. Print that also!

A few years ago (noun phrase), a movie (subject) based on the battle (phrase) of the Alamo (phrase) was (to-be verb) made (subject complement).

P + IC (with two phrases embedded within it)

A producer (subject) turned (verb) the Trojan War (direct object) into a movie (phrase).

IC + P

Historical movies (subject) are (to-be verb) popular (subject complement).

IC

Punctuating Simple Sentences

Simple sentences are easy to punctuate because you only need to remember a few rules:

1. A simple sentence with no phrases requires only a period at the end.

I left work early.

2. When a phrase comes before the independent clause, you follow it with a comma.

Late last night, I heard a screen door slam.

3. When a phrase comes after an independent clause, you don't need a comma.

A taxi took my old man.

Simple sentences are very useful, but compound sentences let you show relationships between ideas.

Compound Sentences

A compound sentence is two or more independent clauses and may include phrases. You can combine independent clauses using

- Coordinating conjunctions
- Conjunctive adverbs
- Correlative conjunctions

Because the punctuation is different for each, you need to know the difference.

You can find a list of these terms on the following pages:

- Coordinating conjunctions, pp. 44–45
- Conjunctive adverbs, pp. 45–46
- Correlative conjunctions, p. 46

> **TIP**
> It is absolutely essential that you learn the words in these lists because the difference between using a comma and a semicolon is based on whether it follows a coordinating conjunction or a conjunctive adverb.

Coordinating Conjunctions

Coordinating conjunctions combine independent clauses to make compound sentences. Because the list is short, you can easily memorize it:

- and
- but
- for
- nor
- or
- so
- yet

Each of these words indicates a different relationship between the two independent clauses it combines, so choose carefully. These words help your reader understand the relationships between the concepts you are explaining:

- And: in addition to
- But: contrast
- For: as a result of
- Nor: neither
- Or: one or the other
- So: cause and effect
- Yet: thus, as a result of

I like to watch movies, **but** I prefer to read books.

Conjunctive Adverbs

Conjunctive adverbs also combine one independent clause with another. However, because you have many more from which to choose, you can show more sophisticated relationships between ideas:

- accordingly
- furthermore
- meanwhile
- similarly
- also
- hence
- moreover
- still
- anyway
- however
- nevertheless
- then
- besides
- incidentally
- next
- thereafter
- certainly
- indeed
- nonetheless
- therefore
- consequently
- instead
- now
- thus
- finally
- likewise
- otherwise
- undoubtedly

Again, you must choose carefully to ensure that your sentences mean what you intend:

> I don't want to go out to dinner; **instead**, I am learning to cook.
>
> I have a black belt in karate, **but** I am learning Judo.

Correlative Conjunctions

Correlative conjunctions are only used in pairs, and they link grammatically equal units—like independent clauses:

- both-and
- neither-nor
- either-or
- not only–but also
- just as–so
- whether-or

To use a correlative conjunction, place one comma after the first independent clause:

> **Either** you clean your room, **or** you can move out.
>
> **Both** of us rent this apartment, **and** both of us will clean it.
>
> **Not only** are you a slob, **but** you **also** eat my food.

Punctuating Compound Sentences

We use three types of punctuation—periods, semicolons, and commas—to punctuate compound sentences. However, as I said before, in order to know which punctuation mark to use, you must recognize what type of word is combining the clauses you write:

- Coordinating conjunction
- Conjunctive adverb
- Correlative conjunction

Coordinating Conjunctions

To create a compound sentence using a coordinating conjunction, follow these rules:

1. Place a comma after the first clause.
2. Place the coordinating conjunction after the comma.

The formula is simple:

> IC + C + CC + IC = I went on vacation, and I lost my passport.

Conjunctive Adverbs

Unlike coordinating conjunctions, conjunctive adverbs take both semicolons and commas. To use a conjunctive adverb, follow these rules:

1. Place a semicolon after the first independent clause.
2. Place a comma after the conjunctive adverb.

You need an independent clause on either side of the conjunctive adverb in order to use a semicolon and comma. Otherwise you only use commas with the conjunctive adverb.

> IC + Semi + SC + C + IC = I had to stay in Aruba for two extra weeks; however, I didn't mind.
>
> IC = I was, however, short on cash.

Correlative Conjunctions

Like coordinating conjunctions, correlative conjunctions only take a comma. Follow these rules when using them:

1. Place the first correlative conjunction at the beginning of the first clause.
2. Place a comma after the first clause.
3. Place the second correlative conjunction at the beginning of the second clause.

> CC + IC + C + CC + IC
>
> Either I enjoy watching movies, or I listen to music.

Complex Sentences

A complex sentence must have two things—at least one independent clause and at least one dependent clause.

The dependent clause can come first or last. A clause is made independent when you add one of these as the first word of the clause:

- Subordinating conjunction
- Relative pronoun

Subordinating Conjunctions

Below is a list of commonly used subordinating conjunctions:

- after
- if
- though
- although
- in order that
- unless
- as
- now that
- until
- as if
- once
- when

- as though
- rather than
- whenever
- because
- since
- where
- before
- so that
- whereas
- even though
- that
- wherever

> Although I've never been to Aruba, I would like to go.
>
> SC + IC + C + IC
>
> I may take my vacation in June rather than going home for Christmas.
>
> IC + SC + IC

Relative Pronouns

A clause can also be made dependent by the addition of a relative pronoun:

- that
- which
- whom
- what
- who
- whoever
- whatever
- whose
- whomever

> The girl **who** sits next to me is my neighbor.
>
> She just moved in, **which** is why I've never met her.

Punctuating Complex Sentences

Creating complex sentences using subordinating conjunctions allows you to show how one idea is supported by another.

Subordinating Conjunctions

Consider the following rules when using coordinating conjunctions:

1. Add a subordinating conjunction to either the first or second of your independent clauses.
2. If the dependent clause comes before the independent clause, place a comma after it.

> As the many books written about them prove, Bonnie and Clyde were notorious gangsters.
>
> SC + IC + C + IC

3. If the dependent clause is last, you do not need any punctuation but a period at the end.

They captured the public's imagination because they were just two ordinary kids from Dallas.

IC + SC + IC

Relative Pronouns

When you use relative pronouns, how you punctuate is based on whether the information in the clause is essential or extra.

Essential: Use "who" or "that"

1. If the clause is essential but does not refer to a person, use "that" or "who" and do not use commas.

He sent for a doctor **who pronounced the victim dead**.

The only information that identifies the doctor is the fact that she pronounced the victim dead.

IC + (that) DC

Love **that is blind** is less valuable than love **that is unconditional**.

Because we are comparing two types of the same thing, love, the description of each type is essential, so no commas are needed. Also, notice that the dependent clause is embedded with the independent clause:

Subject + DC + To Be Verb + Subject Complement + DC + Subject + To Be Verb + Subject Complement + DC

2. If the clause does not contain essential information, start it with "which" and use commas. Also refer to people as "who" or "whom" whether the information is essential or not.

> Michael, **who lives next door**, found her.

The person who found the victim is identified by his name, so where he lives is not essential.

> Subject + (who) DC + Verb + Object
>
> The black VW bug, **which was at the first dealer**, is a better deal than the yellow VW bug, **which is at this lot**.

The writer has identified each car by its color, so the information about its location in not essential and commas were used.

> Subject + (which) + Linking Verb + Subject Complement + Object of Complement + DC

Compound Complex Sentences

A compound complex sentence is exactly what it sounds like—a combination of a compound sentence with a complex sentence. So it must have these elements:

- At least two independent clauses combined with either a coordinating conjunction, conjunctive adverb, or correlative conjunction.
- At least one dependent clause.

> Some scientists believe the earth's climate is changing (IC) and (CC) more major storms are occurring (IC) because pollution is causing a greenhouse effect (DC).

Punctuating Compound Complex Sentences

The great thing about punctuating compound complex sentences is that you simply use the rules that you have already learned for compound and complex sentences.

Coordinating Conjunction

When you use a coordinating conjunction,

1. Place a comma after the first independent clause.
2. Place the coordinating conjunction after the comma.
3. Place the dependent clause either before or after either independent clause.

> Although pollution may cause global warming, we must ask ourselves if all pollution is responsible or if only human pollution is responsible.

Conjunctive Adverb

When you use a conjunctive adverb,

1. Place a semicolon after the first independent clause.
2. Place a subordinating conjunction after the semicolon.
3. Place a comma after the subordinating conjunction.
4. Follow this with another independent clause.
5. Add a dependent clause before or after one of the independent clauses.

> I suspect only human pollution is responsible; however, I have no data to support my hypothesis because I am not a scientist.

Correlative Conjunction

When you use a correlative conjunction,

1. Place the first correlative conjunction at the beginning of the first independent clause.
2. Place the second correlative conjunction at the beginning of the second clause.
3. Add a dependent clause before or after one of the independent clauses.

Either human pollution is to blame or environmental pollution is to blame because it cannot be both.

Review Exercises

Review 1

Identify each sentence type.

1. Because the workplace is global, we must improve our communication skills.
2. Regardless of your area of expertise, you need to be an effective communicator if you want to move up the career ladder.
3. You must know how to communicate verbally and in writing.
4. Although both skills are important, most employers rank writing as the most important skill, so you must develop your skills as a writer.
5. Whether you are connecting internally with colleagues and executives or externally to clients, the way you write can either boost or hamper your progression within the organization.

Review 2

Identify the phrases, dependent clauses, and independent clauses in each sentence.

1. Because the workplace is global, we must improve our communication skills.
2. Regardless of your area of expertise, you need to be an effective communicator if you want to move up the career ladder.
3. You must know how to communicate verbally and in writing.
4. Although both skills are important, most employers rank writing as the most important skill, so you must develop your skills as a writer.
5. Because you are connecting internally with colleagues and executives or externally to clients, the way you write can either boost or hamper your progression within the organization.

Review 3

Correct the punctuation in the following sentences.

1. Your skills as a writer apply to more than just writing emails, because business is all about presentation.

2. Owners aim to set up an effective online presence; and, that online presence requires content.
3. Online content helps potential customers discover the company and its products so to attain this goal, companies create websites, blogs, and social media accounts.
4. Quality content is a decisive factor here, therefore a person, who can present business in the best light and convince people to buy products or services, is an irreplaceable employee.
5. It is time to improve your business communication skills, otherwise, your coworkers will leave you behind.

Answer Key

Review 1

Identify each sentence type.

1. Because the workplace is global, we must improve our communication skills.

   This sentence is complex.
2. Regardless of your area of expertise, you need to be an effective communicator if you want to move up the career ladder.

   This sentence is compound.
3. You must know how to communicate verbally and in writing.

   This sentence is simple.
4. Although both skills are important, most employers rank writing as the most important skill, so you must develop your skills as a writer.

   This sentence is compound complex.
5. Whether you are connecting internally with colleagues and executives or externally to clients, the way you write can either boost or hamper your progression within the organization.

   This sentence is complex.

Review 2

Identify the phrases, dependent clauses, and independent clauses in each sentence.

1. Because the workplace is global (DC), we must improve our communication skills (IC).

The subordinating conjunction "because" makes the clause "because the workplace is global" dependent. The next clause, "we must improve our communication skills," is an independent clause that contains the phrase, "our communication skills," which acts as the direct object of "improve."

2. Regardless of your area of expertise (P), you need to be an effective communicator (IC) if you want to move up the career ladder (DC).

   "Regardless of your area of expertise" is a phrase because it has no verb; because of your expertise, what? The phrase modifies the independent clause, which is combined with a dependent clause using the subordinating conjunction "if."

3. You must know how to communicate (phrase as direct object) verbally and in writing (phrase acting as indirect object) (IC).

   The phrase "how to communicate" is the direct object of the verb "know" because it answers the question, What must you know? "Verbally and in writing" is the indirect object of "communicate" because it answers the question, How must you communicate?

4. Although both skills are important (DC), most employers rank writing as the most important skill (IC), so you must develop your skills as a writer (IC).

   Because it begins with the subordinating conjunction "although," the clause "although both skills are important" is dependent. The next independent clause finishes its meaning and is combined with the last independent clause by the coordinating conjunction "so."

5. Because you are connecting internally with colleagues and executives or externally to clients (DC), the way you write can either boost or hamper your progression within the organization (IC).

   "Because you are connecting internally with colleagues and executives or externally to clients" is dependent because it begins with the subordinating conjunction "because." Its meaning is completed by the independent clause that follows.

Review 3

Correct the punctuation in the following sentences.

1. Your skills as a writer apply to more than just writing emails, because business is all about presentation.

   The comma after "emails" should be deleted because the dependent clause comes AFTER the independent clause.

2. Owners aim to set up an effective online presence; and, that online presence requires content.

   Change the semicolon after "presence" to a comma, and remove the comma after "and." "And" is a coordinating conjunction, so it only takes a comma.

3. Online content helps potential customers discover the company and its products, so to attain this goal, companies create websites, blogs, and social media accounts.

   Because "so" is a coordinating conjunction combining two independent clauses, a comma is needed after the first independent clause.

4. Quality content is a decisive factor here, therefore a person who can present business in the best light and convince people to buy products or services is an irreplaceable employee.

   Because "therefore" is a conjunctive adverb, a semicolon goes after the first independent clause, and a comma goes after "therefore."

5. It is time to improve your business communication skills, otherwise, your coworkers will leave you behind.

   Because "otherwise" is a conjunctive adverb, a semicolon goes after the first independent clause, and a comma goes after "otherwise."

Agreement

When we think about agreeing, we think about sharing the same opinion with someone else. Actually, grammatical agreement isn't that different. When we say a sentence agrees, we mean that the elements in the sentence are either all singular or all plural, all first, second, or third person. Specifically, we need to understand

- Subject-verb agreement
- Noun-antecedent agreement

Because you are already very familiar with subjects and verbs, we'll start there.

Subject-Verb Agreement

As you already know, every sentence has both a subject and a verb. When we are making sure our subjects and verbs agree, that's what we focus on. We can ignore any phrases or objects.

Let's look at some examples:

> Until the audit ends, I (subject) will be (verb) in the office every day.
>
> Accounting (subject), a growing field, requires (verb) a strong understanding of math.

Subjects can be both singular and plural:

- Someone/all
- Child/children
- Business/businesses
- Project manager/project managers

Verbs take their form from the subject, so a singular subject must have a singular noun or vice versa:

- Someone is/all are
- Child runs/children run
- Business grows/businesses grow
- Project managers manage/project managers manage

On the surface, this might seem simple, but it is easy to get confused when phrases come between the subject and the verb.

Pronoun-Antecedent Agreement

A pronoun is a word that replaces a noun. Antecedents can come before or after the pronouns that replace them. The antecedent is the word for which the pronoun stands:

> The dog (antecedent) buried **its** (pronoun) bone.
>
> Mary moved out of **her** apartment.

Types of Pronouns

Personal Pronouns	
Definition:	Stands for a person or thing
Examples:	I, me, mine, our, you, your, he, she, it, its, him, his, her, they, them, their, and theirs
In action:	She (pronoun) is my supervisor (antecedent).

Indefinite Pronouns	
Definitions:	Does not refer to a specific person or thing and doesn't require an antecedent
Examples:	another, any, each, few, many, some, nothing, one, anyone, everyone, everybody, everything, someone, something, either, and neither
In action:	Some (pronoun) of you (antecedent) aren't listening. Nothing (pronoun) will ever get done if we (antecedent) don't stop wasting time.

Reflexive Pronouns	
Definition:	Ends with "self"; person who initiated the contact
Examples:	myself, yourself, oneself, themselves, ourselves, yourselves
Usage:	The engineer (antecedent) didn't run the experiment himself (pronoun). You (antecedent) aren't doing yourself (pronoun) any favors.

Intensive Pronouns	
Definition:	Emphasizes a noun or pronoun that comes right before it; has the same form as reflexive pronouns
Examples:	myself, yourself, oneself, themselves, ourselves, yourselves
Usage:	The athlete (antecedent) herself (pronoun) admitted that she hadn't trained hard enough.

Interrogative Pronouns	
Definition:	Begins a question and does not require an antecedent
Examples:	who, which, what, whom, whose, whoever, whatever, whomever, whichever
Usage:	Who (pronoun) wrote the proposal? Whatever (pronoun) you decide is fine with me.

Demonstrative Pronouns	
Definition:	Identifies a particular thing or group
Examples:	this, that, these, those
Usage:	This (pronoun) is my project (antecedent). That (pronoun) is your responsibility (antecedent).

Reciprocal Pronouns	
Definition:	Shows a mutual relationship
Examples:	each other (two), one another (more than two)
Usage:	We (antecedent) need each other (pronoun).
	The members of the team (antecedent) need one another (pronoun).

Relative Pronouns	
Definition:	Begin a relative clause
Examples:	who, whom, which, that
Usage:	I gave the kitten to the girl who lives next door.

 **IMPORTANT** When you don't know the gender of your subject, you can use a plural antecedent with a singular subject: **The teacher left their books behind**.

Not all antecedents are singular; some are compound.

Compound Antecedents

Compound antecedents can take three forms, and the form determines whether the antecedent takes a singular or plural pronoun.

We will start with the forms that take a singular pronoun:

Compound Antecedents That Take a Singular Pronoun
Two types of compound antecedents take singular pronouns:

1. A compound antecedent that refers to one thing:

> In 1983, Christina McCauliffe, a **teacher and an astronaut** (compound antecedent), lost **her** (pronoun) life aboard the *Challenger*.

2. Two or more antecedents joined by "or" or "nor":

> **Neither McAuliffe nor the American public** (antecedent) was prepared for **her** (pronoun) untimely death.

Compound Antecedents That Take a Plural Pronoun
Two types of compound antecedents take plural pronouns:

1. Two or more antecedents joined by "and":

> **Mike and John** (antecedent) finished **their** (pronoun) exam.

2. A singular antecedent followed by a plural antecedent:

> Neither **I** (singular antecedent) nor my friends (plural antecedent) brought **our** (pronoun) rain gear.

The Basic Rule
All pronouns can be either singular or plural, but if the pronoun is singular, the antecedent must be singular, or vice versa:

> **Do this**
> **The doctors** (plural antecedent) finished **their** (plural pronoun) rounds.
>
> **Don't do this**
> **Neither** (pronoun) **movies nor books** (antecedent) **appeal** (verb) to me.

The verb takes the singular form because the compound antecedent includes the word "or."

Yes **Those** (plural demonstrative pronoun) **were** (verb) **good times** (antecedent).

Because the pronoun and antecedent are plural, the verb must be plural.

Yes **What** (interrogative pronoun) is **Michael** (singular antecedent) doing?

No The **students** (plural antecedent) **himself** (singular reflexive pronoun) **were** (plural verb) glad to end the semester.

Because the antecedent is plural, the pronoun must be as well. "The students **themselves**" is correct.

Apostrophes

Apostrophes have two primary purposes: to indicate a contraction and to show possession.

To Indicate a Contraction

Contractions are combinations of two words into one word. Contractions are normally used in informal writing. The most common contractions combine these words:

- Will not = won't
- Cannot = can't
- Would not = wouldn't
- Is not = isn't
- Are not = aren't
- It is = it's
- Would have = would've
- Could have = could've

In most situations, it's fine to use contractions. They are less formal, but they also give your writing a more approachable style.

You can also use apostrophes to show possession.

To Show Possession

There is the sort of possession that you understand in real life—I own a dog—and there is grammatical possession. Don't get the two confused. Grammatical possession is not always logical because grammatically, inanimate objects and even concepts can possess things. For example:

- Heart's desire
- Two months' salary
- One week's vacation
- Employees' cafeteria

Whether you place the apostrophe before or after the "s" is determined by whether the noun doing the possessing is singular or plural.

Possession

Singular	Plural
boy's hat	boys' hat
animal's DNA	animals' DNA
company's policy	companies' policy
child's game	children's game

When working with nouns that end in "s," even though they are singular, you can either place the apostrophe after the s or use an apostrophe s:

Possession of Words Ending in "S"

Singular	Plural	Plural
Chris' project	Chris's project	
Boss' day	Boss's day	Bosses' day
Marcus' job	Marcus's job	
bus' route	bus's route	busses' route

Quotations Marks

You may be familiar with the use of "air" quotes when you speak, but you may not be as familiar with the use of quotation marks when writing. Quotation marks have many uses:

- To set off direct quotes
- To set off some titles

- To set off words used for emphasis or in special ways
- To indicate non-English words

To Set Off Quotes

The most common use of quotation marks is to set off direct quotes—material that you take directly from another source. Basically, you place a quotation mark before the first word of the quote and after the last word of the quote:

According to NASA, "On January 28, 1986, *Challenger* broke apart shortly after launch. All seven crew members were killed."

TIP
Look closely. Did you notice that you place a comma after the phrase that introduces the quote? Also, the period at the end of the sentence is placed inside the quotation mark.

"They included Christina McAuliffe," NASA remembers, "a teacher, who was aboard as part of a program to make the experience of space flight better known to the public."

TIP
Look closely. If you place material that is not part of the quote within the middle of the quote, it is surrounded by commas.

The *Challenger* disaster seriously impacted the future of the shuttle program: "After the *Challenger* disaster, NASA canceled this program and suspended all shuttle flights."

TIP
Look closely. When you introduce a quote with a complete sentence, you place a colon (:) after the sentence that introduced the quote.

> "Astronauts returned to space on September 29, 1988, aboard the shuttle *Discovery*," said NASA officials.

> **TIP** Look closely. When the introductory material comes after the quote, you place a comma inside the quotation mark after the quote.

You also use quotation marks to identify some titles.

To Set Off Titles

While titles of long works, movies, books, and plays are italicized, titles of short works, or shorter works within a larger work (such as the chapter of a book), are placed in quotation marks:

- Articles: "Beware of the Blob"
- Essays, short stories, short poems, and song lyrics: "Brooklyn Kids"
- Chapters or sections of books: "Strategies for Writing"
- Episodes of radio or TV shows: "The Chicken and the Egg"

To Set Off Words Used for Emphasis or in Special Ways

Sometimes we need to draw attention to a word, show we are defining it, or show that it is non-English:

> She thinks she's so "cool."
>
> The word "elite" is often misused.
>
> It is difficult to define "kairos."

With Other Punctuation

The type of punctuation used with quotation marks determines the placement of the punctuation and whether it is part of the quote. If the quote ends in any of the following, the mark of punctuation goes inside the quotation mark:

- Exclamation point

- Dash
- Question mark

> The movie "Guess Who's Coming to Dinner?" was recently remade.

If the exclamation point, dash, or question mark is not part of the quote, then it goes outside the quotation mark:

> Have you read "Choose Something Like a Star"?

Colons

Colons are used to introduce quotes, lists, and explanations. Because we've already talked about using colons with quotes, we won't cover it again.

To Introduce Lists and Series

A list or series is normally introduced by a complete sentence that is followed by a colon:

> We need to buy the following supplies for our backpacking trip: flashlights, a tent, and sleeping bags.

> We visited the following locations: Dallas, Anchorage, Phoenix, and Honolulu.

To Introduce Explanations

Sometimes a sentence is immediately followed by an explanation. In such a case, a colon separates the statement from its explanation:

> She worked hard for one reason: to attend college.
>
> The Civil War had one cause: the disagreement over the right to own slaves.

Assess—Correctness

1. Which of the following options best describes the parts of this sentence?

    Today, we will study rhetoric.

    a. Today, we (subject) will study (transitive verb) rhetoric (direct object).

    b. Today (subject), we will study (transitive verb) rhetoric (direct object).

    c. Today, we (subject) will study (intransitive verb) rhetoric (adjective).

    d. None of the above.

2. Which of the following options best describes the parts of this sentence?

    Rhetoric was taught in ancient Greece.

    a. Rhetoric (subject) was (transitive verb) taught (direct object) in ancient Greece.

    b. Rhetoric (subject) was (linking verb) taught (subject complement) in ancient Greece.

    c. Rhetoric (subject) was (intransitive verb) taught (adjective) in ancient Greece.

    d. None of the above.

3. Which of the following options best describes the parts of this sentence?

    Isocrates was one of the first teachers.

    a. Isocrates (subject complement) was (linking verb) one of the first teachers (subject).

    b. Isocrates (subject) was (transitive) one of the first teachers (direct object).

    c. Isocrates (subject) was (linking verb) one of the first teachers (subject complement).

    d. None of the above.

4. Which of the following options best describes the parts of this sentence?

    Sadly, the Greeks expelled him.

a. Sadly, the Greeks (subject) expelled (transitive verb) him (direct object).

b. Sadly (subject), the Greeks (direct object) expelled (transitive verb) him.

c. Sadly, the Greeks (subject) expelled (linking verb) him (direct object).

d. None of the above.

5. Which of the following options best describes the parts of this sentence?

He died alone.

a. He (subject) died (transitive) alone (adjective).

b. He (subject) died (intransitive) alone (direct object).

c. He (subject) died (intransitive) alone (adjective).

d. None of the above.

6. The following is a dependent clause: When we exchange information and ideas

a. True

b. False

7. The following is a dependent clause: In the workplace

a. True

b. False

8. The following is an independent clause: The most common communication is written communication.

a. True

b. False

9. The following is a clause: Such as memos and emails

a. True

b. False

10. The following is a phrase: Transmitting information

a. True

b. False

11. Which sentence is punctuated correctly?

a. Good listening skills support the sharing of information in an effective way, and will boost overall communication in the workplace.

b. Good listening skills: support, the sharing of information in an effective way and will boost overall communication in the workplace.

c. Good listening skills support the sharing of information in an effective way and will boost overall communication in the workplace.

d. Good listening skills support the sharing of information, in an effective way and will boost overall communication in the workplace.

e. None of the above.

12. Which sentence is punctuated correctly?

a. Many companies understand the importance of constructive criticism, but it's also important to provide employees with positive feedback to boost communication and employee work effort.

b. Many companies understand the importance of constructive criticism but it's also important to provide employees with positive feedback to boost communication and employee work effort.

c. Many companies understand the importance of constructive criticism; but, it's also important to provide employees with positive feedback to boost communication and employee work effort.

d. Many companies understand the importance of constructive criticism, but, it's also important to provide employees with positive feedback to boost communication and employee work effort.

e. None of the above.

13. Which sentence is punctuated correctly?

a. Because face-to-face meetings provide an opportunity for clarification, they encourage employees to communicate with others in a more effective way and they reduce stress.

b. Because face-to-face meetings provide an opportunity for clarification they encourage employees to communicate with others in a more effective way, and they reduce stress.

c. Because face-to-face meetings provide an opportunity for clarification; they encourage employees to communicate with others in a more effective way, and they reduce stress.

d. Because face-to-face meetings provide an opportunity for clarification, they encourage employees to communicate with others in a more effective way, and they reduce stress.

e. None of the above.

14. Which sentence is punctuated correctly?
    a. When they, work well together, teams thrive.
    b. When they work well together, teams thrive.
    c. When they work well together, teams thrive
    d. When they work well together teams thrive.
    e. None of the above.

15. Which sentence is punctuated correctly?
    a. Team-building exercises also boost morale.
    b. Team-building exercises also boost morale
    c. Team-building exercises also boost morale . . .
    d. Team-building, exercises also boost morale.
    e. None of the above.

Engage—Correctness

The following passage contains errors in grammar and punctuation. How many can you find?

Different types of writing have different purposes. Creative writing is meant to entertain, consequently, creative writers take all sorts of liberties with there sentence structures and word choices. We do not read poetry or novels to learn how to perform tasks; but for the pure pleasure of the words and they're artistic affect. Literary works are not meant to have one unambiguous meaning.

> Professional writing is meant to inform and instruct very few people will chose to read directions for designing a website. You will read them only when you want or need to design a website, you will not want to read more than is absolute necessary.
>
> Reader's rightly expect instructions to be free of ambiguities. They simply want to achieve their goal quickly and correctly. According to some people, this style is what make informational writing different from other types of writing. The style of informational writing is always different from the style of fiction; but its the audience that determines the style choices a writer make. What really makes informational writing different from other types of writing is it's focus on meeting its audiences needs.

To complete this assignment:

1. Cut and paste the document into Microsoft Word.
2. In Microsoft Word, turn on "Track Changes."
3. In the document, correct any errors you find with "Track Changes" turned on.
4. Save your document to your computer, and upload it to this discussion.
5. After making your revisions, view and comment on at least three of your classmates' posts and help them identify any errors they missed.

Apply—Correctness

The following document contains several errors in grammar, punctuation, and word choice. Please find and correct each error. Follow this process:

1. Cut and paste the document into Microsoft Word.
2. Highlight each error you find.
3. Insert a blank page.
4. Correct each error and place them on the blank page.

Note: Many of the errors you will find can be corrected using more than one method. I will accept any that are correct.
5. Save your work.
6. Submit it.

Six Steps for Writing Professional Emails

If you're not sure how to start an email, these five steps can help you craft a professional message:

Identify Your Goal

Before you write an email, ask yourself what you want the recipient to do after they've read it. Once you've determined the purpose of your email, you can ensure everything you include in your message supports this action. For example, if you want the recipient to review a report you've attached, let them know what the report is, why you need them to review it, what sort of feedback you need, and when you need the task completed.

Consider Your Audience

When you compose an email message, make sure your tone matches your audience; for example, if you're emailing a business executive you've never met, keep the email polished and free of any jokes or informalities. On the other hand, if you're emailing a colleague with whom you have a good relationship, you might use a less formal, more friendly approach.

Keep It Concise

Your audience might have little time to read through your email. Make it as brief as possible without leaving out key information. Try not to address too many subjects at once, as this can make your message lengthy, challenging to read, and difficult to take action on. When editing your email, take out any information that's irrelevant to the topic you're addressing. Use short, simple sentences by removing filler words and extraneous information. This will make your note shorter and easier to read.

Proofread Your Email

An error-free email demonstrates diligence and professionalism. Before you send an email, take a moment to check for any spelling, grammar, or syntax errors. Also, double-check to ensure you've included any attachments you may have referenced in your message. If it's an important email to critical stakeholders, you might ask your direct supervisor or a trusted colleague to read over it before you send it.

Use Proper Etiquette

Include a courteous greeting and closing to sound friendly and polite. Additionally, be considerate of the recipient and their time. For example, unless it's an emergency, avoid emailing a contact asking for something after-hours or while they're on leave.

Remember to Follow Up

Most people receive several emails per day, so they might miss or forget to respond to your message. If the recipient hasn't replied within two working days, consider reaching back out with a friendly follow-up email.

Jennifer Herrity's (2023) article "How to Write a Professional Email (With Tips and Examples)" on Indeed.com is an excellent reference on writing professional emails.

Assignment Rubric

	Superior	Above Average	Average	Below Average	Failing
Content	20 points	15 points	10 points	5 points	0 points
	Includes all of the required elements of the assignment.	Includes all of the required elements, though some are under-developed.	Includes most of the required elements.	Includes some of the required elements.	Does not include all of the required elements.

	Superior	*Above Average*	*Average*	*Below Average*	*Failing*
Style	20 points	15 points	10 points	5 points	0 points
	The writing is clear and concise and avoids unnecessary use of passive constructions.	The writing is clear and concise and generally avoids unnece-ssary use of passive construc-tions.	The writing is mostly clear and concise and mostly avoids unnecessary use of passive construc-tions.	The writing is occasionally clear and concise but does not avoid unnece-ssary use of passive construc-tions.	The style is inappropriate or unclear.
Design	20 points	15 points	10 points	5 points	0 points
	The document has a clear visual hierarchy and the writer uses appropriate methods of presentation such as lists and tables.	The document has a clear visual hierarchy and the writer uses some appropriate methods of presentation such as lists and tables.	The document has a basic visual hierarchy and the writer occasionally uses appropriate methods of presentation such as lists and tables.	The document's visual hierarchy is weak and the writer doesn't use appropriate methods of presentation such as lists and tables.	The document has no visual hierarchy.
Structure	20 points	15 points	10 points	5 points	0 points
	The organization of the document is clear and logical and makes strong use of topic sentences and transitions.	The organization of the document is generally clear and logical and makes some use of topic sentences and transitions.	The document has an organization and occasionally uses topic sentences and transitions.	The structure is weak and the writer rarely uses topic sentences or transitions.	The document has no structure.
Correctness	20 points	15 points	10 points	5 points	0 points
	The document has no errors.	The document has 2–3 errors.	The document has 4–5 errors.	The document has 6–7 errors.	The document has 8 or more errors.

Style

Learning Objectives
- Use strong subjects and verbs.
- Make your subject the actor.
- Keep actor and action together.
- Eliminate unnecessary words.
- Make appropriate word choices.

Learn—Style

Introduction

Different types of writing have different purposes. For example, creative writing is meant to entertain. Consequently, creative writers take all sorts of liberties with their sentence structures and word choices.

Look at this example:

> Nelson cannot dance, which is to say he will not, for all dancing is now standing in place and letting the devil of the music enter you, which takes more faith than he's got. (Updike 1981, 303)

Strictly speaking, this example makes one point: Nelson won't dance because he is too unsure. However, the use of figurative language reveals a great deal about Nelson's state of mind.

We do not read poetry or novels to learn how to perform tasks but for the pure pleasure of the words and their artistic effect. Literary works are not meant to have one unambiguous meaning. Professional writing, on the other hand, is meant to inform and instruct. Very few people **choose** to read instructions for designing a website. You only read them when you want or need to design a website, and you will not want to read more than is necessary. Readers rightly expect instructions to be free of ambiguities. They simply want to achieve their goal quickly and correctly. Using a professional writing style is one way of ensuring that your writing is as clear as possible. But what is writing style?

At its most simple level, style is how formal or informal our language is. Look at these examples:

1. See ya later at meeting. Ping me if ??

2. I look forward to seeing you at the meeting this afternoon at 2. Feel free to email me if you have any questions.

The first example is very informal. The writer leaves out words, uses slang, and replaces words like "questions" with symbols. This level of informality can lead to confusion and isn't a good choice for professional purposes.

The second example is more formal and easier to understand.

Style choices like the level of formality, the words you use, and the order of those words all affect how well, or even if, your writer will understand what you are writing. In this chapter, we discuss methods for creating a clear writing style that will allow you to meet your readers' needs.

Use Strong Subjects and Verbs

Strong sentences have strong subjects that appear at the beginning of the sentence. Strong subjects are important because they help you meet your readers' expectations by immediately giving them an important piece of information—who is doing what. When the subject of our sentence has no meaning, the reader will struggle to find meaning:

What is this sentence trying to say?

> There has been job loss connected by engineers to the introduction of labor-saving technology.

What is the subject of this sentence? Did you think it was "job loss"? It makes sense for **job loss** to be the subject of the sentence because that is what the sentence seems to be about, but actually the grammatical subject of this sentence is **there**.

> There (subject) has been (to-be verb) job loss (subject complement).

Because the subject **there** has no meaning, this sentence is difficult to understand without a lot of unnecessary work. It is never a good idea to use **there** as the subject of a sentence. It is also best to have human actors as subjects whenever possible. Look at this revision:

> Engineers have connected labor-saving technology to job loss.

Strong subjects should do the action in the sentence.

Make Your Subjects Actors

Generally speaking, it is best to have people act as the subject of sentences when possible. For example:

> It is a well-known fact that companies need technical writers.

The subject of this sentence is "it." But who and what are really doing the action?

> Companies need technical writers.

The second sentence is shorter and clearer because a strong subject, "companies," is doing the action, "needing."

Frequently, when sentences have weak subjects, the sentence also has a passive verb, which is why it is better to use active voice when you can.

As we learned earlier, what type of verb a sentence contains will determine whether the sentence has a subject that is capable of action.

Active Constructions

Transitive and intransitive verbs normally follow subjects that are capable of action—people or things:

> Recently, a tiger (subject) in a Russian zoo abandoned (transitive) her cubs (direct object).
>
> Luckily, a large dog (subject) adopted (transitive) them (direct object).
>
> Without the dog's help, the cubs (subjects) would be dead (intransitive).

Each of these sentences has an active construction because the subject of the sentence is doing the action of the verb:

Subject	Verb
tiger	abandoned
dog	adopted
cubs	would be dead

Copular Constructions

Linking verbs and to-be verbs allow us to create sentences that define or describe—a copular construction:

Basic Copular Constructions

> The sky **is** blue.
>
> He **looks** nervous.

The subject of a sentence that uses a linking verb or to-be verb can be a person, thing, object, or concept. The subject does not need to be capable of acting because the to-be verb does the action of saying the subject is or is like the subject complement:

> Global warming is (to be) a weather phenomenon (subject complement).
>
> Some scientists believe global warming is (to be) a natural phenomenon (subject complement).
>
> Other scientists believe that it is (to be) human made (subject complement).
>
> Either way, it seems (linking verb) likely (subject complement) to change our weather patterns for many years.

Sentences that use to-be and linking verbs are not passive even though they contain to-be verbs. Sentences that follow a subject-verb-subject complement structure allow writers to compare one thing to another or describe one thing as another. These types of copular constructions are very useful when describing or defining abstract concepts because they allow writers to compare the unknown to the known:

> A black hole in space is like a drain in a bathtub.

So unless you have a specific reason for using passive voice (which we discuss next), you should use one of these constructions:

Construction	Example
Subject + transitive verb + object	The astronaut attempted to repair the space station.
Subject + intransitive verb	She succeeded.
Subject + linking or to-be verb + subject complement	A black hole in space is like a tunnel in the earth.

As with all of your communication choices, the answer to whether to use passive voice depends on the rhetorical situation.

For some audiences, purposes, and reasons, passive voice is the best choice. For example, you might need to let your coworkers know that the coffeemaker is broken, but you don't necessarily need to identify who broke it. It was you! In other contexts, however, such as instructions, passive is not a good choice because the reader needs to know who should do what:

> The screw should be attached.
>
> Attach the screw.

But before we can decide when to use passive voice, we have to learn to recognize it.

Recognize Passive Constructions

We call some verb structures "passive" because within the grammatical structure of the sentence, no actor is present to do the action of the verb, or the actor is present in the sentence but is not the subject of the sentence:

> The data was collected by the astronauts on the space shuttle.

In this sentence, the subject is "data." The action of the sentence is "collected," but the subject cannot do the action. "Astronauts" should be doing the collecting, but they are in the prepositional phrase that ends the sentence. Look at this revision:

> The astronauts on the space shuttle collected the data.

In this version of the sentence, "astronauts" is the grammatical subject of the sentence, and they do the action of "collecting." Passive constructions must meet three criteria:

1. The grammatical subject of the sentence is not capable of acting.

2. The sentence contains a to-be verb (am, is, are, was, were, be, been, being, have been).
3. The to-be verb is followed by a past participle (a verb with an -*ed* form; irregular verbs are an exception to this).

Look at the previous example:

> The data (subject not capable of action) was (to-be verb) collected (past participle) by the astronauts on the space shuttle.

As you can see, it meets all three criteria to be passive voice. Look at the five sentences below and determine which are examples of passive voice.

1. Yesterday, I discovered that my department's copier didn't work.
2. Apparently, the copier had been broken.
3. I didn't want to take the blame for the broken copier, but I also didn't want to report the problem.
4. The copier is expensive, and the repair will be costly.
5. The issue will have to be reported by someone other than me.

Don't Make This Mistake

NOTE Remember, a passive construction must meet all three of the criteria listed earlier, not just one or two. Other sentence structures contain to-be verbs, but because they may have an actor or not contain a past participle, they are not passive constructions.

Look at these examples:

> 1. Flu is a dangerous illness.
>
> 2. My sister was ill with flu last year.
>
> 3. She was hospitalized.

Each of these sentences contains a to-be verb, but they do not contain past participles. In this case, we have a subject, a to-be verb, and a subject complement. These sentences DO NOT have passive constructions.

When Is Passive Voice a Poor Choice?

Passive constructions are poor choices for two reasons:

1. They do not answer the question "Who did it?"
2. They are wordy.

In many cases, who did the action of the sentence is as important or more important than what was done.

Look at these examples:

> The election **was won** by Chris Taylor.
>
> The meeting on Monday at 4:00 **must be** attended by all employees.
>
> The young boy **was saved** by the quick actions of the firefighter.

All of these sentences can be revised to reduce the number of words and make it clear who it was and who did what:

The bolded verbs make these sentences active

> Chris Taylor **won** the election.
>
> All employees must **attend** the meeting Monday at 4:00.
>
> The firefighter's quick actions **saved** the young boy.

In each of these sentences, we know who was or is responsible for the action of the verb.

Sometimes, however, what was done is more important than who did it, or we may not know who did it. We may even want to protect the person who did it or want to avoid laying blame. Look at these examples:

> My book was stolen from my office. The proposal was rejected.

If something is stolen, we usually don't know who stole it, so we have to use passive voice. In the second sentence, we might want to avoid saying who rejected the proposal in order to keep the process objective. Another way to make sentences strong is to keep the actor and the action side by side.

Keep Actor and Action Together

As we discussed previously, depending on the sentence type, a sentence may contain one or more subjects as well as multiple verbs. A sentence can also contain one or more phrases. Look at this example:

> During the last space mission (phrase), the Russian (modifier) astronaut (subject), who had been living on the space station (relative clause) for several months (phrase), attempted to repair (verb) the malfunctioning (modifier) space station.

In this sentence, a relative clause and a phrase come between the subject and the verb. Look at this revision:

> During the last space mission (phrase), the Russian (modifier) astronaut (subject) attempted to repair (verb) the malfunctioning (modifier) space station. She (subject) had been living (verb) on the space station for several months (phrase)

By placing the subject and verb together, we have strengthened the sentence. We can also confuse a sentence's meaning by separating the subject and the verb with unnecessary information or by placing the subject somewhere besides the beginning of the sentence:

> In the bright sunshine (phrase) stood (verb) an old mansion (subject) surrounded (verb) by a moat and wall (phrase), strong and proud (phrase), almost as in the feudal times (phrase).

This sentence contains many phrases and modifiers that obscure its meaning, and the verbs come before the subjects. Look at this revision. We now have a subject doing the action of the sentence:

> A moat and wall surrounded the old feudal mansion.

When writing, less is almost always more! This is true of single words as well.

Eliminate Unnecessary Words

Writers often use more words than are necessary. This problem can have several causes:

- Unnecessary repetition
- Weak subjects
- Weak verbs
- Not letting the verb do the action of the sentence

Unnecessary Repetition

Sometimes, writers repeat words for effect—I came, I saw, I conquered—but professional writing is about function, not effect. Look at this sentence:

> I can go on and on talking about my eagerness to learn more and more about writing.

Do the extra **on** and extra **more** add to the sentence's meaning, or do they just get in the way of the writer's point? Also, the writer uses the verb **go** rather than letting **talking** do the action of the subject. Let's get rid of the extra words:

> I could keep talking about my eagerness to learn more about writing.

This revised sentence makes the point more clearly and succinctly.

Weak Subjects

Look at this sentence:

> There are many things that I want to learn from this book.

The subject of this sentence is **there**, and the verb is **are**. Because **are** is a to-be verb, it is followed by the subject complement **things**. So this is the core sentence:

> There are things.

Because both the subject and the complement have no meaning, the sentence has no meaning. The reader must look to the dependent clause that comes last to find out what the sentence is trying to say:

> That I want to learn from this class.

Because it begins with the relative pronoun **that**, the clause is dependent, but it does have an actor, **I**, doing something, **want**.

Let's revise the sentence by making **I** the subject and placing it first:

> I want to learn many things from this class.

Now we have someone doing something. Passive constructions and verbs with no action also cause wordiness.

Weak Verbs

As we discussed earlier, sometimes you will want to use passive voice. However, is this sentence one of those times?

> The desire to write was planted in me by my high school English teacher.

The subject of this sentence is **desire**, and we know that desire was **planted** by the writer's teacher. Why not let the teacher be the subject of the sentence so they can do the action?

> My high school teacher planted a desire to write in me.

By revising this sentence to remove the passive voice and add an actor as the subject, we removed the extra words and made the point much clearer. We also make our sentences wordy when we turn verbs into nouns.

Verbs Should Be Actions

Sometimes, writers take verbs and use them as nouns. In this sentence, **investigate** is being used as a noun rather than a verb:

> The investigation (noun) of the murder was conducted by the police.

Because we made **investigate** a noun, **investigation**, we have to add another verb, **conducted**, to do the action. Adding the extra verb makes the sentence wordy and less accurate. Let's turn **investigation** back into a verb:

> The police investigated (verb) the murder.

Now the sentence is shorter and more accurate. Look at this sentence:

> The choice (noun) of a school is a decision made by college students every day.

In this sentence, the writer makes the verb **to choose** into a noun. How would you revise it?

> Every day, students choose colleges.

See the difference? Structure is not the only way to build a strong sentence. You also have to choose the best words.

Making Appropriate Word Choices

We can replace many words with other words that mean almost the same thing. For example, look at these lists of synonyms:

Use
utilize, operate, employ

Exercise
set in motion, put to use, work, wield

Yes
affirmative, aye, true, correct, certainly, surely, agreed

Hypothesis
question, postulation, supposition, theory, opinion

Given that you have a large number of words to choose from every time you write a single sentence, the question is, How do you make the right choice? You always choose the word that will communicate most effectively to your audience. For example, match the best word choice to the audience:

Word choices

- Hypothesis
- Question
- Opinion

Audiences

- Sixth-grade science students
- Law students
- College chemistry majors

Answers for matching word choice to audience

Word Choice	Audience
Hypothesis	Chemistry major
Question	Sixth-grade science students
Opinion	Law students

When deciding what word to use, remember these guidelines:

Choose the word the audience expects

When you ask a friend if she wants to go to the movie, you probably don't expect her to say, "Aye." "Yes" or "sure" would be fine. However, if you were taking an official vote at a meeting, the chair will say, "All in favor, say aye." Context matters.

Most of the time simple is best

Very rarely do you need to use "utilize" rather than "use." Those sorts of twenty-dollar words sound pretentious, and they don't add any additional meaning.

Use technical terms when appropriate

If you are writing for a group of experts, use technical terms. For example, if you are writing for accountants, use the term "accrue." They understand that term and its professional meaning. On the other hand, don't use that word in common conversation: "If I continue to accrue more shoes, I will need a bigger closet." Really?

Use consistent terms

Many writers believe that using synonyms rather than repeating the same word multiple times adds variety to their writing. No. When you refer to the "report" in one sentence, the "paper" in the next, and the "memo" in the last, you leave your reader wondering if you are talking about one document or three!

Simple doesn't mean simplistic

Simple means concise and elegant. Simplistic means dull, plain, and lacking. Simple writing uses clear words that convey their meaning with as little potential for misinterpretation as possible. However, in order to convey a clear meaning, you must also use precise words.

For example, if you are writing instructions for baking cookies, you can't tell your reader to "warm the oven." What does "warm" mean? Does it mean 200 degrees, 400 degrees, 500 degrees? You must be specific and say, "Heat the oven to 350 degrees."

If you were writing a safety manual for water safety professionals, you wouldn't say, "Cover your face up with something when you work with dangerous chemicals." Cover your face with what? A bandana? A ski mask? You would tell them to wear a respirator. Because of their training, they will be familiar with this term.

Assess—Style

1. Strong sentences should begin with strong subjects and have human actors whenever possible.
   a. True
   b. False

2. What is the difference between transitive/intransitive verbs and linking/to-be verbs?
   a. Transitive and intransitive verbs normally follow subjects that are capable of performing the action in real life.

    b. Transitive and intransitive verbs are actions that can literally be done.

    c. Transitive and intransitive verbs describe the subject and often indicate passive voice.

3. Which three criteria must be met for a sentence to be passive? Select all that apply.

    a. The grammatical subject is not capable of performing the action.

    b. The sentence contains a to-be verb.

    c. The sentence has a past participle (verb ending in "ed") after a to-be verb (with some exceptions).

    d. The sentence separates the subject and the verb with a phrase.

    e. The thing capable of performing the action appears at the end of the sentence.

4. Which of the following are passive voice? Select all that apply.

    a. The lawn was mowed by my brother.

    b. Our collection is admired by several people.

    c. Keith was unhappy.

    d. The puppy is sleeping.

5. A sentence is harder to understand when the subject and verb are separated.

    a. True

    b. False

6. Which sentences could be rewritten to have the actor and action closer together? Select all that apply.

    a. The tortoise, which had lived in this lake for twenty years, suddenly went missing.

    b. Late in the evening, Sally, exhausted from the long walk home, noticed that she'd forgotten her cell phone back at school.

    c. I couldn't believe that my grandpa went on a solo ski trip without telling us.

7. Scientific and professional writing is about function, not effect.
   a. True
   b. False

8. What can cause sentences to become wordier than necessary? Select all that apply.
   a. Using unnecessary repetition
   b. Not making the subject the actor
   c. Using passive voice
   d. Not letting the verb do the action of the sentence

9. What does it mean for a subject to be "an actor"?
   a. The grammatical subject of a sentence would be able to perform the action described in the sentence in real life (the action might not be the grammatical verb).
   b. The verb of a sentence makes sense given the subject.
   c. The grammatical subject of a sentence would be able to have the action described in the sentence done to it in real life.

10. Which sentences have subjects that are actors? Select all that apply.
    a. There are many things that I want to learn from this course.
    b. My CDs were cleaned and reorganized.
    c. She went crowd-surfing at the concert.
    d. I cleaned and reorganized my CDs.
    e. What was expected was not this.
    f. Sandy shredded his new chew toy in ten minutes.

11. Which sentences use verbs as nouns that could be better used to do the action of the sentence? Select all that apply.
    a. The investigation of the incident was conducted by the city police.
    b. The performance of the team was fantastic.
    c. The kitty's stalking of the bird was silent.
    d. Our gaming disturbed his sleep.
    e. My coach knew just want to do.

12. In professional writing, it's better to use the same word to repeatedly refer to something rather than using several synonyms.
    a. True
    b. False

13. In professional writing, using big words and technical jargon is preferred over plain language.
    a. True
    b. False

14. What are good guidelines to follow when choosing the words you will use in your writing? Select all that apply.
    a. Use plain words.
    b. Use words with a clear, precise meaning.
    c. Use terms suitable for your audience.
    d. Use highly technical words.
    e. Use the simplest words possible, even if it sacrifices some of your meaning.
    f. Use words that no one other than your audience will know.

Engage—Style

How would you review these sentences?

Provide a revision for each, then respond to at least three of your classmates and let them know how they did.

1. There are books that may be dismissed with a single reading.
2. It is seldom that a student does equally well in all of his or her subjects.
3. The discovery of the American continent was made by Columbus, a native of Italy.
4. There are times in the life of everyone when new and strange things occur with such rapidity that one is hardly able to catch one's breath.
5. It is probable that the Southern states would not have begun the Civil War had the Southern people realized the great wealth and resources of the North.
6. Every day I make observations of other writers.

7. I am more prepared than I have ever been before to effectively and successfully write professional documents professionally.
8. The report was written by the engineers.

Apply—Style

The following assignment is based on this scenario:

Your work in the claims department for Pets Are People Too. Recently, your company had to recall a very popular cat tower because it kept collapsing and posed a safety risk to both cats and their people. However, because the tower is expensive—$800— people who didn't purchase the product are illegally asking for refunds. In order to ensure they are only offering refunds to legal customers, the company is changing its refund policy.

The company's CFO, Chris Craft, drafted the email below to explain the new verification process and asked you to review it. After reading it, you believe the style and tone could be improved:

Dear Refund Requester,
If you actually purchased the Towering Heights Kitty Castle, we apologize sincerely and abjectly for any delay that may have ensued in your ability to receive the refund you legally are owed. If you are one of those people who is trying to game the system, we don't care about you, so stop reading. As you may have determined from the tone of this message, Pets Are People Too has been plagued by a tsunami of fraudulent demands for refunds on the very expensive Towering Heights. As a result, we have suffered epic losses. To mitigate our damage, we are instituting a new system of purchaser verification that requires you to provide the company with certain forms of information in order to receive a refund. If we do not have proof of your purchase, we will not refund your money. If we do not receive proof of purchase within sixty days, we will close your account and assume you do not want your money back. We appreciate our customers and their pets, and hope you will comply with our request.

Sincerely,
Chris Craft

Your Task

For this assignment, complete the following steps:

1. Identify any errors in style and tone in the email.
2. Write a brief memo to Chris that:
   - Summarizes three issues you found. Support your recommendations by citing your course materials.
   - Suggests changes that will address the issues you identified. Support your recommendations by citing your course materials.

As you write, remember to use an indirect approach. You are giving Chris bad news.

Assignment Rubric

	Superior	Above Average	Average	Below Average	Failing
Content	20 points	15 points	10 points	5 points	0 points
	Includes all of the required elements of the assignment.	Includes all of the required elements, though some are under-developed.	Includes most of the required elements.	Includes some of the required elements.	Does not include all of the required elements.
Style	20 points	15 points	10 points	5 points	0 points
	The writing is clear and concise and avoids unnecessary use of passive con-structions.	The writing is clear and concise and generally avoids unnecessary use of passive con-structions.	The writing is mostly clear and concise and mostly avoids unnecessary use of passive con-structions.	The writing is occasionally clear and concise but does not avoid unnecessary use of passive con-structions.	The style is in-appropriate or unclear.

	Superior	*Above Average*	*Average*	*Below Average*	*Failing*
Design	20 points	15 points	10 points	5 points	0 points
	The document has a clear visual hierarchy and the writer uses appropriate methods of presentation such as lists and tables.	The document has a clear visual hierarchy and the writer uses some appropriate methods of presentation such as lists and tables.	The document has a basic visual hierarchy and the writer occasionally uses appropriate methods of presentation such as lists and tables.	The document's visual hierarchy is weak and the writer doesn't use appropriate methods of presentation such as lists and tables.	The document has no visual hierarchy.
Structure	20 points	15 points	10 points	5 points	0 points
	The organization of the document is clear and logical and makes strong use of topic sentences and transitions.	The organization of the document is generally clear and logical and makes some use of topic sentences and transitions.	The document has an organization and occasionally uses topic sentences and transitions.	The structure is weak and the writer rarely uses topic sentences or transitions.	The document has no structure.
Correctness	20 points	15 points	10 points	5 points	0 points
	The document has no errors.	The document has 2–3 errors.	The document has 4–5 errors.	The document has 6–7 errors.	The document has 8 or more errors.

Structure

Learning Objectives
- Write effective introductions.
- Write effective supporting paragraphs.
- Write effective conclusions.
- Use transitions in sentences.
- Use transitions between sentences and paragraphs.

Learn—Structure

What Is Coherence?

Cohesive writing is sticky writing. What makes it stick?

Every idea is clearly related to the one that came before; the ideas stick together. Sticky writing starts with a sticky structure. Everything you write that you intend to publish (let someone else read) must have a structure.

Even the shortest of emails needs a structure; otherwise, it's going to sound like stream of consciousness. Have you received any of those emails lately? However, before you worry about the structure, you must choose your approach.

Whether a document is short or long, whether it's an email or formal report, you have two choices: direct approach or indirect approach.

Direct Approach

When you use a direct approach, you get directly to the point. You don't start with any polite chitchat or formalities. You simply state the point you want to make and go from there. Americans are very comfortable with the direct approach, but not every culture is. If you are writing to someone from another country, say China, you need to consider their preferences regarding the approach that you use because many cultures prefer a highly polite, indirect approach for all writing situations. A great deal of information about this topic is available on the internet, so do your homework. When should you use the direct approach?

- When giving good news. Everyone likes to get good news, so get to it.
- When the information or request is simple and neutral. For example, if you are reminding your team members that you have a meeting scheduled for the next day, no one is going to be upset or concerned, so you can get to the point.
- If someone requested information from you. If you are responding to a direct request for information, the other person understands the context, so you can be direct.

The direct approach doesn't always work. If the communication situation is more complicated, you may need to use an indirect approach.

Indirect Approach

When you use an indirect approach, you begin with a buffer intended to help you gain the goodwill or cooperation of the reader. Sometimes we have to tell people things they don't want to hear, but if we do it persuasively and demonstrate that we are empathetic to their position, we can increase the chance of a positive outcome and decrease the chance of an unpleasant escalation.

Use the indirect approach when:

- You are giving bad news. No one wants to be told that they didn't get the promotion, or the raise, or the sale. Unfortunately, no one wins all of the time, and you will have to share bad news. By creating a buffer, you give yourself the opportunity to point out the positive first. You can also acknowledge the person's feelings.
- You can demonstrate the positive side of the situation.

Let's imagine that your company is initiating a new dress policy because people are getting a little too casual. It's your job to send out a company-wide email making everyone aware of this change. Which approach is better?

Dress Code Example 1

New Dress Code Rules
Because too many of you are coming to work looking unprofessional in yoga pants, jeans, and flip-flops, we are initiating a new dress policy.

Starting Monday, everyone must wear the following:

. . .

Dress Code Example 2

Dress for Success Initiative
Thanks to everyone for their hard work. Our numbers for the last quarter were up, and our future is looking good.

To continue our positive growth, we are beginning a new dress for success initiative. Our clients respond to how we look, so let's look as professional as possible. Our new initiative starts in two weeks.

Below is a list of clothing guaranteed to demonstrate our professionalism:

Both paragraphs provide the same information: you may have to change how you dress. However, the way that message is shared is very different.

The first paragraph demonstrates no gratitude to the employees and directly insults them by saying they dress like slobs. The new plan is called a "code" and it comes with "rules." Both of those words have unpleasant baggage.

The second paragraph begins positively and explains that the new "initiative" is intended to benefit the employees. No criticism is given, and no blame is cast. Also, a rational reason is given for the initiative: our clients react to how we look. Because everyone benefits when the company succeeds, employees will be likely to cooperate happily. Let's look at the basic structure of both approaches.

Direct

1. Reason for writing
2. Background information if needed
3. Request and/or information
4. Closing

Indirect

1. Buffer
2. Reason for writing
3. Background information if needed
4. Request and/or information
5. Closing

Once you choose your approach, you need to create your structure. To create a sticky structure, you must do the following:

- Write an effective introduction.
- Provide relevant, supporting paragraphs with strong topic sentences and transitions.
- Write a strong conclusion.

The introduction is perhaps the most important part of any document because it prepares the reader for what follows. If the introduction is not effective, the reader may not read any further.

Writing an Effective Introductory Paragraph

If you want to encourage your reader to keep reading, you need to write an interesting and relevant introduction. You will give the readers important information that they need in order to understand the rest of your document. All introductions must include a sentence that states the main idea and a road map to guide the reader throughout the rest of the document.

The main idea or thesis of a document should state the purpose of the document. Why are you writing this document? Stating the main idea up front creates context for readers to understand the details that follow in your document. If you don't provide the necessary context and main idea for your readers, then they may have to reread the passage. If that is the case, you have failed as the writer. Your readers should always have a clear understanding of your main idea after they read the introduction.

In addition to including an effective introduction, you need to provide your readers with a road map, so they know what information you plan to discuss in the remainder of the document. A road map clearly sets the readers' expectations by briefly outlining the rest of the document.

The road map should state the main sections of the document. Doing so introduces the readers to the way you have organized your document and puts them at ease because they know what is coming up in the document. Road maps do not have to be lengthy; they simply have to state the order of the rest of the document.

Here is an example of a well-written introduction, but yes, the topic is just for fun:

> According to Dr. Lame Duck, who has a PhD in zombiology, the likelihood of people under the age of 18 becoming zombies grows each day. In an article he published about zombies in *Zombie Weekly*, he said, "I fully believe that 25 percent of the population under 18 will be infected by zombititis by the year 2020." Teachers need to be aware of this zombie epidemic.
>
> In this article, teachers can learn about how they can
>
> - Identify a zombie
> - Identify the symptoms of zombititis
> - Prevent zombititis.

This introduction gives readers a clear understanding of who the target audience is (teachers), why the writer is writing this article (thesis), and how the document is organized (road map). If the readers were zombies and wanted to know how to survive and spread zombititis to others, this article would not help them. Understanding purpose and audience is crucial to writing a good introduction.

Writing Coherent Supporting Paragraphs

As a writer, your goal is to write paragraphs that provide the reader with unity and coherence—the cornerstone to a well-written document.

All supporting paragraphs should have:

- A topic sentence
- Supporting sentences
- A concluding sentence (oftentimes transitions to the next paragraph)
- Transitions

If written correctly, these sentences combine together to create coherent paragraphs that flow together, so your reader can easily understand the supporting content you are providing in the document.

Topic Sentence

The first sentence in a paragraph is your topic sentence and works like a purpose statement for the paragraph. This sentence states the main idea of the paragraph. The supporting sentences must support the topic sentence. If not, your paragraph lacks coherence. Think of each paragraph as a mini-paper that has a unifying idea. Next, connect each sentence in the paragraph logically to the preceding sentence(s).

Supporting Sentences

Strong supporting sentences unify a paragraph. If a sentence does not fit with the topic sentence, you have three options for correcting it:

1. Rewrite your topic sentence.

2. Delete the sentence.
3. Find another more suitable place for it in your paper.

Oftentimes, deleting something from a document can be painful, but for the sake of coherence, you need to do it. Also be careful that your supporting sentences are not repetitive. You can say the same thing in many different ways. You may find that you have to delete a sentence or two because you've repeated the same information in two different ways. To avoid repetition, you must carefully revise your paper.

Concluding Sentence

In addition to strong, cohesive supporting sentences, you need to conclude each paragraph with a sentence that sums up what you've just talked about and, in some cases, introduces the new topic for the next paragraph. A sentence that restates the old information and introduces new information that will appear in the next paragraph is called a transition sentence. Here are examples of each type:

Transitional sentence
Now that you understand passive constructions, we will talk about nominalizations.

Concluding sentence
Now that you have read this guide, you should have a basic understanding of the principles of professional communication.

Transitions

As you write, you will use transitions: words or phrases that help bring two ideas together. Transitional words and phrases help to provide the reader with the unity and coherence we mentioned earlier. Certain words help continue an idea, indicate a shift of thought or contrast, or sum up a conclusion. The following list of words will help you to write paragraphs that will pull your sentences and paragraphs together.

Showing Similarity

- likewise
- similarly
- moreover

Showing Contrast

- instead
- even so
- on the other hand
- yet
- on the contrary
- otherwise
- however
- but
- nevertheless

Showing Results

- accordingly
- because
- hence
- therefore
- as a result
- consequently
- since
- thus

Continuing an Idea

- also
- first (second, third, etc.)
- similarly
- then
- additionally
- in addition
- because
- besides
- likewise
- clearly
- furthermore
- and
- moreover

Drawing Conclusions

- as a result
- in brief
- to summarize
- finally
- in conclusion

Pointing out Examples

- for example
- to illustrate
- for instance

Showing Emphasis and Clarity

- above all
- again
- in other words
- nonetheless

- after all
- besides
- specifically
- that is

Conceding a Point

- granted that
- to be sure

- of course
- admittedly

Indicating Time

- after
- as soon as
- at last
- before long
- in the meantime
- while
- next
- once
- subsequently
- soon
- immediately

- afterward
- at first
- before
- finally
- later
- meanwhile
- now
- previously
- until
- then

Separating Sections of a Paragraph That Is Arranged Chronologically

- first . . . second . . . third
- generally . . . furthermore . . . finally
- in the first place . . . also . . . lastly
- to be sure . . . additionally . . . lastly
- basically . . . similarly . . . as well

Signaling a Conclusion

- therefore
- hence
- in conclusion
- indeed

- this
- in final analysis
- in final consideration

Choosing the right transitions is as important as using them. Transitions will help your document flow better and provide unity for the overall document.

Writing a Strong Concluding Paragraph

A conclusion sums up a document and signals that the discussion has been completed. A concluding paragraph should restate the main idea (purpose) and summarize the main points that you made in the document. The conclusion should not introduce new material that is irrelevant to your document.

For example, the conclusion for the zombititis article might look like this:

> The number of zombification cases has risen each day. In addition, there is a growing fear that 25 percent of the youth will become zombies by 2020. However, Dr. Lame Duck has discovered the causes of the disease and how to prevent its spread. Hopefully, this article has shown teachers how to identify the symptoms of zombititis, treat the symptoms of zombititis, and prevent zombititis. Perhaps, with a better understanding, teachers can help to stop the spread of zombification and the number of zombies will begin to drop.

This conclusion does a good job of repeating the main sections discussed in the article and reiterating the main idea: how teachers can help to stop the spread of zombification.

The conclusion is the last impression a reader has of your document. Be sure to take the time to write a strong conclusion.

As the writer, you should give some serious thought to your conclusion and help your readers know what you want them to take away from reading your document. A strong conclusion may be the difference between receiving funding for a research project or not.

Assess—Structure

1. Introductions are always optional.
   a. True
   b. False

2. Which of the following items does an effective introduction NOT include?
   a. A statement of purpose
   b. A road map
   c. At least one interesting quote
   d. A transitional sentence

3. This an effective introduction to an email:

   Hey, hey, hey. Please read this email carefully.
   a. True
   b. False

4. The following statement accurately describes a topic sentence: The first sentence in a paragraph is your topic sentence, and it works like a purpose statement for the paragraph. This sentence states the main idea of the paragraph.
   a. True
   b. False

5. What is the purpose of a supporting sentence? Choose each option that fits.
   a. To provide examples that support the topic sentence
   b. To introduce a new topic to keep the paragraph interesting
   c. To provide specific details
   d. To provide evidence to prove your statement is true, such as quotes or paraphrases from outside sources
   e. To provide contrasting opinions

6. Which of the following sentences uses the transitional word "because" most effectively?
   a. I like pizza because I like tacos.
   b. I have scheduled a meeting of our team because we will meet Monday at 10:00 am.

    c. I have scheduled a meeting of our team because we need to finish our project.

    d. Because I have scheduled a meeting, it is Monday at 10:00 am.

7. Which of the following does NOT describe what a conclusion does?

    a. Introduce a new idea

    b. Restate the main idea (purpose)

    c. Summarize the main points that you made in the document

    d. If appropriate, let the reader know how to get more information

8. Transitions will help your document flow better and provide unity for the overall document.

    a. True

    b. False

9. The transitional word in the following sentence shows what relationship between ideas?

    To finish this project, we must meet with the software engineers. Next, we should user test the software.

    a. Cause and effect

    b. Chronology

    c. Comparison

    d. Contrast

10. Is this statement true or false?

    Every paragraph, with the exception of your conclusion, should end with a transitional sentence.

    a. True

    b. False

Engage—Structure

The following example, "How to Write Concise, Accurate Sentences," has issues with its structure:

How to Write Concise, Accurate Sentences

Every word we write can be misinterpreted by the reader. Why? Every word in the English language has multiple meanings: Sick can mean "I have the flu" or "This new song is amazing." Warm: It is 30 degrees (if you live in Alaska, this could be warm); it is 85 degrees (if you live in Texas, this could be warm). The purpose of professional and technical communication is to be as accurate and objective as possible. Our goal is to eliminate confusion and the possibility for misinterpretation. How do we do that? In this exercise, we will look at sentences I pulled from past assignments. Each sentence has some type of issue. We will learn how to identify the issue. We will learn how to correct it. To understand what a sentence does incorrectly, we need to identify the sentence's structure. To do that, we can follow these steps: Identify the subject and verb. Identify each independent clause. Identify each dependent clause. Identify any phrases. Once you have done this, revise the sentence based on these principles. To write effective sentences, we should keep four principles in mind. Make the subject a human/thing capable of doing the action. Use an active verb. Place the most important information first. Eliminate fluff (unnecessary information).

Your Task

Now that you have read the article, complete the following steps:

1. Choose three principles from the list below:

   - Includes an effective introduction
   - Includes effective supporting paragraphs
   - Includes an effective conclusion
   - Uses transitions within sentences
   - Uses transitions between sentences

2. Write a memo in which you discuss how effectively the example follows the principles you chose.

3. Use examples from the example to support your claims.
4. Use your readings to support your claims.
5. Follow best practices for writing memos.
6. Post your memo.
7. Respond to three of your classmate's posts. Give them feedback on both their analysis of the example and the quality of their memo.

Apply—Structure

Please read the following scenario.

> Because you have taken a course in professional communication, your supervisor has asked you to write a series of memos that address writing issues. These memos will be given to the members of your department so that they can improve their own writing. Your first memo will address the topic of professional structure.

Your Task

For this assignment, you will write the memo on professional structure. Follow these tips:

1. Focus on three issues.
2. Use your class readings to back up your recommendations.
3. Provide original examples.
4. Follow the practices for effectively structuring a professional document when writing your memo.

Assignment Rubric

	Superior	Above Average	Average	Below Average	Failing
Content	20 points	15 points	10 points	5 points	0 points
	Includes all of the required elements of the assignment.	Includes all of the required elements, though some are under-developed.	Includes most of the required elements.	Includes some of the required elements.	Does not include all of the required elements.

	Superior	*Above Average*	*Average*	*Below Average*	*Failing*
Style	20 points	15 points	10 points	5 points	0 points
	The writing is clear and concise and avoids unnecessary use of passive con-structions.	The writing is clear and concise and generally avoids unnecessary use of passive con-structions.	The writing is mostly clear and concise and mostly avoids unnecessary use of passive con-structions.	The writing is occasionally clear and concise but does not avoid unnecessary use of passive con-structions.	The style is in-appropriate or unclear.
Design	20 points	15 points	10 points	5 points	0 points
	The document has a clear visual hierarchy and the writer uses appropriate methods of presenta-tion such as lists and tables.	The document has a clear visual hierarchy and the writer uses some appropriate methods of presentation such as lists and tables.	The document has a basic visual hierarchy and the writer occasionally uses appropriate methods of presentation such as lists and tables.	The document's visual hierarchy is weak and the writer doesn't use appropriate methods of presentation such as lists and tables.	The document has no visual hierarchy.
Structure	20 points	15 points	10 points	5 points	0 points
	The organization of the document is clear and logical and makes strong use of topic sentences and transitions.	The organization of the document is generally clear and logical and makes some use of topic sentences and transitions.	The document has an organization and occasionally uses topic sentences and transitions.	The structure is weak and the writer rarely uses topic sentences or transitions.	The document has no structure.
Correctness	20 points	15 points	10 points	5 points	0 points
	The document has no errors.	The document has 2–3 errors.	The document has 4–5 errors.	The document has 6–7 errors.	The document has 8 or more errors.

Graphics

Learning Objectives
- Design an effective page layout.
- Create a visual hierarchy.
- Integrate text and graphics.
- Use Microsoft Word efficiently.

Learn—Professional Design

How you visually present your words is almost as important as the words themselves. This is true for several reasons:

- Good design makes good information even more useful.
- Because of technology, we no longer communicate with just words.
- When you demonstrate good design, you let your readers know that you are a communication specialist.

Your words are important, but honestly, no one wants to read one more word of a set of instructions or a report than is absolutely necessary. Good design allows you to take large pieces of information and present them in manageable chunks, which allows your readers to find what they need and get there quickly.

Educated readers have expectations. Laboratory reports, for instance, follow a standard design format. If you don't know and use that format, you will not meet your readers' expectations, and they will doubt the credibility of your work. So in short, design is more than just making it pretty.

Good design makes your words more effective.

Page Layout—Creating an Effective Design

We can divide the principles of page layout into three parts:

1. Creating a visual hierarchy
2. Chunking information
3. Creating useful graphics

However, before we start talking about these principles, let's discuss basic design vocabulary.

Design Terms

Serif font
Serifs are the small "feet" on the ends of letters in fonts such as Cambria, Times New Roman, and Georgia.

Sans serif font
Sans means without, and sans serif fonts do not have serifs. Sans serif fonts include Calibri, Ariel, and Corbel.

Left justified
When all of the text on a page is aligned on the left margin, the text is left justified.

Right justified
When all of the text on a page is aligned on the right margin, the text is right justified.

Right ragged
When the text on the page is not filled with white space to make it aligned but instead ends naturally, it is right ragged.

Left hanging
When you left justify your headings but indent all of your body text, you have a left-hanging format.

Bullet
Small solid black dots placed before items in a list are called bullets.

Headers

Standard information that appears outside of the margin at the top of each page of a document is called a header. Page numbers and chapter titles frequently appear in headers.

Footers

Standard information that appears outside the bottom margin of each page of a document is called a footer. Footers frequently contain page numbers or the author's name.

Indent

The space created when you move the first line of a paragraph a half inch to the right is an indentation.

Font size

Fonts come in different sizes, typically measured in points (pt or pts) by most word processors. Points such as 9, 10, and 11 are common for body text in print documents.

Visual hierarchy

When you use font sizes and weights to indicate the hierarchy of information, you have created a visual hierarchy.

Level-one headings

The highest level of heading, it should be the largest heading size; 16-point font size is a good starting point on print documents.

Second-level headings

The second-highest level of heading; 14-point font size is a good starting point on print documents.

Third-level headings

The third level heading; use 12-point font size, bold, as a starting point on print documents.

The typographical suggestions above are just that—suggestions. There are many ways to format a document, but these are generally safe options. We will use these suggestions throughout the rest of this chapter.

Look at how the example memo below uses each of these different formatting styles.

A left-justified memo

To: Professional Writing Students
From: Dr. R
Date: September 15, 2020
Re: How to Write Memos

Some of you have had some questions about how to format and organize a memo, so in this memo, I will address your questions. We'll start by talking about how to format a memo.

When we format memos, or any professional document, we want to follow some basic best practices. These practices weren't adopted because they make a document look nice, or because a bunch of tech writers just decided they like doing it that way. Experts have adopted these practices because they make the information accessible to the reader by

- Breaking the information into manageable chunks
- Using headings to visually organize the different topics
- Organizing the information in a persuasive manner

Header information
No indent | left justified | right ragged | single spaced

First and second paragraphs
No indent | left justified | right ragged | single spaced | bullets

Bulleted Lists
Space after previous bullet | no indent | left justified | right-ragged | single spaced

CAUTION Notice I didn't put a colon after "by"? Only put a colon after a complete sentence that introduces a list; otherwise, don't use any punctuation.

Best Practices for Designing a Short Document

When we design memos, emails, and short reports, we want to follow some basic best practices. These practices weren't adopted because they make a document look nice or because a bunch of tech writers just decided they like doing it that way. Experts have adopted these practices because they make the information accessible to the reader by

- Breaking the information into manageable chunks
- Using headings to visually organize the different topics
- Organizing the information in a persuasive manner

When we read a document on a screen, the lighting makes the letters appear to shimmer. Consequently, the simple form of a sans-serif font is easier for someone to read.

Left justify, right ragged

When we say a piece of text is justified, we mean each line starts or stops in the same space. When we say ragged, we mean each line stops or starts in a different place. Because we read from left to right, justifying the left margin makes it easy for our eyes to go to the right place. However, if we also justify the right margin, the computer will randomly add filler spaces to each line. These spaces create inconsistent gaps between words that make it harder for us to read. Our eyes "trip" over those gaps like we would trip over a crack in the sidewalk. Some publishers prefer to fully justify the content of their books, which is why this book uses full justification.

Single space within paragraphs; add a space between paragraphs

Single spacing paragraphs allows us to visually show which information goes together, while the space between paragraphs lets us easily see where one ends and another begins. Do NOT indent the first line of a paragraph.

When we indent the first line of a paragraph, we create another of those stumbles for the readers' eyes.

Use headings to create a visual hierarchy

When we use headings, we create an outline of the entire document that allows our readers to skim and find what they need. Headings should be larger than the body text, so we can find them easily:

Level One Heading
16-point font

Level Two Heading
14-point font

Level Three Heading
12-point bold font

You don't need to use headings for your introduction or your conclusion—just for paragraphs that cover specific topics.

Use a bulleted list to emphasize important information

If you are providing a list of something (ingredients, names, requirements, etc.), a bulleted list is a good way to do it. Bulleted lists are a powerful design tool, but be careful you don't turn a document into one long list!

Introduce every list with a sentence

A list without context can confuse your reader, so always introduce the list with a sentence.

Use tables to consolidate information

I have placed the best practices into a table because the table lets me present the information concisely, and it keeps it organized.

Now let's talk about how to create a visual hierarchy.

Creating Visual Hierarchy

All information is not created equally. In any given document, regardless of its length, some information is more important than other information.

If we can visually separate the most important information from the least important information, we can help our readers prioritize effectively.

The most effective way to create a visual hierarchy is by using headings:

Visual Element	Size	Capitalization and Alignment
Title	18-point Calibri	Capitalize all words except prepositions, articles, or coordinating conjunctions.
Level one headings	16-point Calibri	Capitalize all words except prepositions, articles, or coordinating conjunctions.
Level two headings	14-point Calibri	Capitalize all words except prepositions, articles, or coordinating conjunctions.
Level three headings	12-point Calibri, bold	Capitalize all words except prepositions, articles, or coordinating conjunctions.
Body text	12-point Calibri	Left justified, right ragged.

Once we have created our visual hierarchy, we can use it to organize our information into manageable chunks.

Chunking Information

When we give our readers pages and pages of unbroken words, we make their job very difficult because we are ensuring that they have to read every word to find any meaning. We also make it difficult for them to remember what they read because we overload them with too much information at one time.

When we present information in smaller chunks, we give readers the opportunity to start and stop as they choose. This makes reading a less frustrating process, and it increases retention.

To chunk information effectively, follow these tips:

- Avoid using more than four levels of headings, when possible.
- Always use a sentence to introduce a bulleted list.
- Make headings parallel (use the same grammatical structure).
- Use lists for emphasis only. When the entire document becomes a list, it is more likely to become a distraction.

- Single space within chunks.
  - Include a paragraph space before and after chunks of information.
- Include a paragraph space after headings.
- Left justify/right ragged.
- Use one-inch margins on all four sides.
- If a document is more than one page in length, include page numbers.

Look at the document below. Does it follow the principles we've discussed?

Original Memo

> Sample Survey
>
> Dear Faculty Member,
> We will launch a program this semester to test a new kind of evaluation. Because you are getting this letter, you are one of the faculty who have been chosen for the trial evaluation.
>
> When you receive the evaluation (a copy of it is attached), we want you to do a number of things. Please announce that the evaluation will be given and urge students to attend class that day. If some students are absent the day you give the evaluation, give those students an evaluation the next class period. For this trial evaluation, it is imperative that every student in the section complete a survey. Have someone else administer the survey—either a colleague or your department administrator. Be sure you are not present during the time the students are completing the survey. Have the person who gave the survey collect all of them and place them back in the envelope. This should be sealed in front of the students. The person who sealed the envelope should return it to 104 Jones Hall. Give the envelope to Mickey Smith. Sign the sheet to indicate that you have returned your trial survey.

A quick glance at this document tells us only two things: it is about a sample survey, and it is in the form of a letter. Neither piece of information tells the reader anything useful. Furthermore, because the majority of the information is contained in a single paragraph, readers must read every word to learn anything. By adding a visual hierarchy to this document, and making the embedded instructions accessible, we can greatly increase the usability of this document:

Revised Memo

Launch of New Survey

We will launch a program this semester to test a new kind of survey. You have been chosen to administer the trial survey. Please follow the instructions below:

How to Administer the Survey

After you receive the envelope containing copies of the trial survey, do the following:

- On the day before the survey, announce the date you will give the survey.
- Inform students that they must take the survey. Students absent the day you give the survey must take it the next class period.
- Choose someone to administer the survey—either a colleague or your department administrator
- On the day of the survey, leave the room so your representative can give the survey.

Before you leave, ask them to do the following:

1. Pass out the surveys.
2. When every student is done, collect all of them and place them back In the envelope.
3. Seal the envelope in front of the students.
4. Ask you to return to class.
5. Return the envelope to 104 Jones Hall.
6. Give the envelope to Mickey Smith and sign the sheet to indicate you returned the trial survey.

How to Get Help

If you have questions or need help, please contact me at *example@example.com*.

Why Is This Better?

This revised version is better for many reasons:

- The headings provide readers with information that allows them to determine exactly what they must do and when.
- The numbered steps inform the reader that the instructions must be completed in a specific order.
- The information is chunked into smaller sections instead of long paragraphs.

I guarantee that the second document will get better results than the first!

Integrating Text and Graphics

"Graphic" is the word we use to refer to any information that is visual rather than textual: drawings, photos, diagrams, tables, and charts. Some graphics, such as tables, do include words, but the words support the visual elements, not vice versa. Graphics are very important. In many cases, we can show more effectively than we can tell.

Which example more clearly explains what a pipette is?

Describe a pipette

With words
A pipette is a long, slender device for transferring liquids. One end is more bulbous than the other, and the other end has a small hole that fluids enter/exit when the bulb is squeezed.

A picture

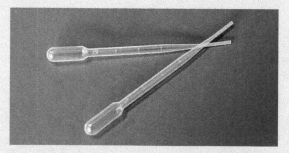

Figure 5.1 Pictures often describe something better than words can.

Because some people learn by seeing and others by reading, it is best to use both words and graphics. However, we only want to use graphics that serve a purpose—to illustrate a necessary piece of equipment, show data trends, or provide specific visual details. Never throw in graphics, especially clip art, just because you can.

When creating graphics, follow these tips:

1. **Only use graphics that serve a purpose.**
   If you are writing about how to place a muzzle on a dog, a photo of someone muzzling a dog would serve a purpose. A picture of a cute puppy would not.
2. **Make the style of the graphic appropriate to the purpose of the document.**
   If you are writing an overview of a surgical procedure for patients, photos of the surgery would not be appropriate. These photos would be too graphic and would scare the readers. Line drawings would be better. Photos would be appropriate for surgical students.
3. **Do not use clip art just because you can.**
   Random clip art is distracting and unprofessional. When possible, use high-quality images or illustrations in appropriate locations within a document.
4. **Label and number all graphics.**
   Use an informative label that describes the graphic.

Labels for Figures

Labels for figures must be aligned with the left margin of the graphic and placed below. Labels for tables must be aligned with the margin of the table and placed above.

Figure 5.2 Dog with a muzzle.

How to label an image

Integrating text and graphics effectively requires you to do more than just copy a graphic onto a page. You must follow the four basic principles of good design.

Four Principles of Good Design

These four principles should direct your design decisions:

- Contrast
- Repetition
- Alignment
- Proximity

Contrast

Contrast means difference, and effective graphics use contrast to draw attention to the most important element in the graphic. We can create contrast using color, size, or placement. In the photo below, the contrast between the white text on the black background draws eyes to the text; some people might not even notice the much darker text in the top half of the picture because it lacks contrast with the black background. A lack of contrast can make it difficult for readers to discern differences between elements, which means that the graphic loses its meaning.

Figure 5.3 Low contrast vs. high contrast.

How Can You Create Srong Contrast?

Use white fonts on dark backgrounds. Use dark fonts on light backgrounds. Use different font sizes.

Repetition

When you reuse the same or similar elements throughout a document, you create repetition, and this creates visual coherence. We can also create visual repetition through consistent use of fonts, colors, and graphic styles. For example, you might decide to use only black-and-white photos in a particular document.

Figure 5.4 Repetition.

How Can You Create Effective Repetition?

- Use a consistent font
- Use a consistent color scheme
- Use consistent placement of text and graphics

Alignment

Types of Alignment

You can use six types of alignment.

Horizontal
Either the left or right (or both) margins are equal. You can apply it across a single column or an entire page.

Vertical
Your text or design elements are lined up with the top and bottom margins on the page.

Edge
Your text and design elements are lined up with each other's top, bottom, or side edges.

Center
Your elements are aligned along a central axis.

Visual/Optical
An element is misaligned because of a rounded element.

Breaking
Breaking the rule for effect; this can be applied to pages, columns, or text frames.

How Can You Create Alignment?

- Use tables
- Left justify large blocks of text
- Only center very small graphics or blocks of text

Proximity

When we use white space to connect or disconnect items on the page, we are using proximity. In other words, items that are close are related, and items that are far apart are not.

How Can You Create Proximity?

- Use less white space to show items are part of the same group.
- Use more white space to show items are part of different groups.
- Embrace white space; it prevents your design from looking crowded and helps direct the reader's eye to key elements by contributing to your visual hierarchy.
- Create a visual hierarchy; group similar items together and create white space. Use contrast and fonts.

Graphics can be very powerful when properly utilized. When improperly used, they often serve as a distraction and can confuse readers.

Incorporating Images

Images should support the surrounding text and be sized so that the reader can discern what the image is and how it relates to the writing. When working with images, keep in mind the final medium for the document. If the document will be printed on a black-and-white printer, perhaps a dark-colored image won't look as good on paper as it does on-screen.

Make Images Accessible

Not all readers can see the images in your writing the same way they can read words. Label images and use "alt text" so screen readers can describe the image for the visually impaired. Alt text is a description that a writer assigns to an image.

Each type of writing software has a different way to add alt text to an image. Most word processors allow you to add alt text from the menu that appears after right-clicking the image.

Alt text has the following benefits:

- Screen readers can describe images to the visually impaired.
- If there is a problem that prevents an image from displaying, its alt text can help the reader understand what is supposed to be in that space.
- Search engines can find documents with images more easily.

Tables, Charts, and Graphs

Tables, charts, and graphs can be very powerful when trying to relay data to the reader. However, to make your tables, charts, and graphs effective, you must

- Label axes.
- Use color effectively.
- Name the figure so it can be listed in a list of tables and figures.
- Provide a short, informative caption describing the data.

Student Attendance in the Professional Writing Lab

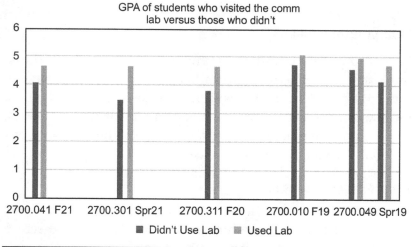

	Didn't Use Lab	Used Lab
2700.041 F21	4.1	4.2
2700.301 Spr21	3.5	4.7
2700.311 F20	3.8	4.7
2700.010 F19	4.8	5.1
2700.049 Spr19	4.6	5
Averages	**4.16**	**4.74**

Assess—Professional Design

1. Which of the following statements does NOT provide a reason why professional design is important?
   a. Good design makes good information even more useful.
   b. Because of technology, we no longer communicate with just words.
   c. When you demonstrate good design, you let your readers know that you are a communication specialist.
   d. It makes documents pretty.

2. This is an example of a serif font:

   Times New Roman
   a. True
   b. False

3. What kind of justification does this paragraph use?
   Educated readers have expectations. Laboratory reports, for instance, follow a standard design format. If you don't know and use that format, you will not meet your readers' expectations, and they will doubt the credibility of your work. So in short, design is more than just "making it pretty." Good design makes it more effective.
   a. Left justified
   b. Right justified
   c. Fully justified
   d. Centered

4. Centered justification is a good choice.
   a. True
   b. False

5. Which statement is most accurate?
   a. Always use right-ragged left justification.
   b. Only use left justification.
   c. Only use right justification.
   d. Only use full justification.

6. Always indent the first line of each paragraph.
   a. True
   b. False

7. Always use the direct approach when giving bad news.
   a. True
   b. False

8. Which statement best describes a visual hierarchy?
   a. It includes photos.
   b. It visually separates the most important information from the least important information using different sizes of headings, so we can help our readers prioritize effectively.
   c. It makes all text the same size.
   d. There is no such thing.

9. Select every statement that is true.
   a. Never have more than four levels of headings.
   b. Always use a sentence to introduce a bulleted list.
   c. Make headings parallel.
   d. Use lists for emphasis only. When the entire document becomes a list, the lists have become a distraction rather than a help.
   e. Single space within chunks.
   f. Space before and after chunks of information.
   g. Space after headings.
   h. Use right-ragged left justification.
   i. Use one-inch margins on all four sides.
   j. If a document is more than one page in length, use page numbers.
   k. All of the above

10. The most effective way to create a visual hierarchy is by using headings.
    a. True
    b. False

Engage—Professional Design

For this discussion, we are going to continue working with the document from the "Style" discussion. Although you worked on the structure, the document still has issues with its design.

How to Write Concise, Accurate Sentences

Every word we write can be misinterpreted by the reader. Why? Every word in the English language has multiple meanings: Sick can mean "I have the flu" or "The new song is amazing." Warm can mean "It is 30 degrees" (if you live in Alaska, this is warm) or "It is 85 degrees" (if you live in Texas, this is warm). The purpose of professional and technical communication is to be as accurate and objective as possible. Our goal is to eliminate confusion and the possibility for misinterpretation. How do we do that? In this exercise, we will look at sentences I pulled from past assignments. Each sentence has some type of issue. We will learn how to identify the issue. We will learn how to correct it. To understand what a sentence does incorrectly, we need to identify the sentence's structure. To do that, we can follow these steps: Identify the subject and verb. Identify each independent clause. Identify each dependent clause. Identify any phrases. Once you have done this, revise the sentence based on these four principles: Make the subject a human/thing capable of doing the action. Use an active verb. Place the most important information first. Eliminate fluff.

Your Task

For this discussion, complete the following steps:

1. Create an effective page design and layout.
2. Create a visual hierarchy.
3. Make the information accessible.
4. Submit the revised document.
5. Respond to three of your classmates' posts.
6. Offer suggestions on the quality of their revision.

Apply—Professional Design

Before you begin, read the following scenario:

> Because you have taken a course in professional communication, your supervisor has asked you to write a series of memos that address different writing issues. These memos will be emailed to the members of your department so they can improve their own writing. This particular memo will address the topic of professional design, layout, and structure.

Your Task

For this assignment, you will write the second memo in the proposed series. You will be writing about professional structure. Your audience is your colleagues. Because this is an imaginary situation, use what you know from your own work and educational experience to analyze your audience. As you write your memo, follow these tips:

1. Focus on how to create an effective page design, create a visual hierarchy, and make information accessible.
   * You are teaching your colleagues how to create a visual hierarchy and make information accessible, so tell them what they need to know and provide examples of how to do it.
   * You are NOT teaching computer skills, so you don't need to tell them how to use Word.
2. Use your class readings to back up your recommendations.
   * Your colleagues need to know that you are the expert, so share what you've learned from your course.
   * You can quote from the course materials, but remember to use quotation marks.
3. Provide original examples.
   * You have already learned how to design a page, so use your own work as examples.

4. Follow the best practices for effectively structuring a professional document when writing your memo.
    - The document you send to your colleagues should not just tell how to design a page.
    - It should also provide an example of how to write an effective memo, so apply the principles you have learned.

Assignment Rubric

	Superior	Above Average	Average	Below Average	Failing
Content	20 points	15 points	10 points	5 points	0 points
	Includes all of the required elements of the assignment.	Includes all of the required elements, though some are underdeveloped.	Includes most of the required elements.	Includes some of the required elements.	Does not include all of the required elements.
Style	20 points	15 points	10 points	5 points	0 points
	The writing is clear and concise and avoids unnecessary use of passive constructions.	The writing is clear and concise and generally avoids unnecessary use of passive constructions.	The writing is mostly clear and concise and mostly avoids unnecessary use of passive constructions.	The writing is occasionally clear and concise but does not avoid unnecessary use of passive constructions.	The style is inappropriate or unclear.
Design	20 points	15 points	10 points	5 points	0 points
	The document has a clear visual hierarchy and the writer uses appropriate methods of presentation such as lists and tables.	The document has a clear visual hierarchy and the writer uses some appropriate methods of presentation such as lists and tables.	The document has a basic visual hierarchy and the writer occasionally uses appropriate methods of presentation such as lists and tables.	The document's visual hierarchy is weak and the writer doesn't use appropriate methods of presentation such as lists and tables.	The document has no visual hierarchy.

	Superior	Above Average	Average	Below Average	Failing
Structure	20 points	15 points	10 points	5 points	0 points
	The organization of the document is clear and logical and makes strong use of topic sentences and transitions.	The organization of the document is generally clear and logical and makes some use of topic sentences and transitions.	The document has an organization and occasionally uses topic sentences and transitions.	The structure is weak and the writer rarely uses topic sentences or transitions.	The document has no structure.
Correctness	20 points	15 points	10 points	5 points	0 points
	The document has no errors.	The document has 2–3 errors.	The document has 4–5 errors.	The document has 6–7 errors.	The document has 8 or more errors.

Problems

Learning Objectives
- Recognize the types of problem/solution documents.
- Understand when to write about a problem and solution.
- Understand how to respond to a problem/solution document.
- Understand how to structure a problem/solution document.
- Write a short problem/solution document.
- Write a longer problem/solution document.

Learn—Problems

Writing to Address Problems

As a professional, you will have to solve problems every day. Some problems you can solve with a quick conversation:

> Would you proofread this email for me?

Other problems you'll need to discuss with your colleagues during a meeting:

> Unless we hire another team member, we won't be able to complete all our projects on time.

And some problems you'll have to write about.

For example, if you are a supervisor, you might need to write a letter documenting a problem with one of your employee's performances. Because personnel issues have to be documented, you would always put these types of problems in writing.

Or perhaps, as in the example above, you feel your department is understaffed, and you want to hire a new member for your team. Any request that involves significant cost—another salary—has to be written down because it has to be approved at multiple levels.

Perhaps your team works with your company's engineers to sell filtration systems to hospitals and care facilities. A hospital won't purchase your product unless you can convince them that not having it is a problem. Because a filtration system costs thousands of dollars, a hospital would want all the details in writing so they can make an educated decision.

Any writing you do involves a certain level of persuasion. Just getting someone to read what you write is an act of persuasion. But writing about problems is one of the most persuasive forms of writing, which makes it challenging.

As with any writing challenge, if you understand the structure and the process, you can write the document. When you write to propose a solution to a problem, you should follow this process:

1. Identify the problem.
2. Convince your readers that your problem is their problem too.
3. Provide a solution.
4. Develop a plan of action.
5. Provide a plan for implementing the solution.

Let's look at each part of the process in more detail.

Identify the Problem

When you write about a problem, you have more information than your readers. After all, you are the one who identified the problem. However, that doesn't mean your readers have the same level of familiarity or that they agree that what you consider a problem actually **is** one.

Consider this scenario.

> You supervise a team of six employees. As the supervisor, it is your job to evaluate each of your team member's performance every six months. In these written evaluations, you are expected to identify any problematic performance issues and suggest a solution.
>
> Unfortunately, one of your team members has been consistently late to work, late to complete tasks, and requesting more than the allowed number of personal days. You have spoken to them about this issue before, but their behavior hasn't changed. When you tried to explain that their behavior was creating problems for the rest of the team, who had to do the work that they weren't completing, they said, "I can't help it. My life is complicated."
>
> Now it is your job to do the following:
>
> 1. Write a review for this employee.
> 2. Convince them their behavior is a problem that is affecting the entire team.
> 3. Gain the cooperation of the employee to correct the issue.

You've identified the problem, but how do you convince your employee to agree with you?

Convince Your Readers the Problem Affects Them

If we want to convince someone that they have a problem, we must look at it from their perspective, not our own.

Let's go back to our scenario.

From your employee's perspective, the problem isn't that they're late and don't get their work done and need days off. The problem is that their life is complicated, and they can't help it.

This might be true, but as the supervisor, you also have to consider how this employee's behavior affects the company.

When team members have to use their time to do the other person's work, they fall behind in their own work. This means the entire department falls behind, which reflects poorly on you. But how do you make this clear to the source of the problem?

Show Empathy

Acknowledge that you understand that outside issues are currently affecting them. Express concern and sympathy. For example, you might say this:

Three Examples Expressing Concern and Sympathy

> Sometimes I had trouble getting my kids to school on time too, which meant I couldn't get myself to work on time.
>
> I talked to some of my kid's parents and found out they have the same problem.
>
> We organized a car pool, which really helped all of us.

This response shows that you understand because you've had the same problem. You also offer a potential solution. Most importantly, you didn't shame or blame.

Explain Your Perspective

You can't just ignore the problem. Even though you are sympathetic, the person's behavior is affecting everyone negatively. If the problem isn't solved, the employee's job will be at risk, and it is only fair that they understand this. You could explain your perspective this way:

> You have always been a considerate member of this team, and I'm sure you don't realize how your problems affect the rest of us.
>
> When you don't get your work done, someone else has to do it. Everyone else is as busy as you, so it's not fair to expect them to do more than they already do.
>
> Also, if our team's productivity goes down, we will all be held accountable, so everyone has to do their best work.

Summarize the Problem

When you summarize the problem, you clearly state what is at stake for everyone:

> We need to work together to develop a solution for improving your work performance so that you can keep your job and no one else is negatively affected.

Provide a Solution

Once everyone agrees that a real problem exists, you can propose a solution to fix it. Your solution must

- Address the issue.
- Be realistic.

Address the Issue

In our scenario, you need to find a solution for your employee's lateness, missed deadlines, and excessive requests for personal days. Your proposed solution could be a simple "You must stop," but that solution won't work. If they could just stop they probably would. You need to analyze the source of the problem and work from there:

- The employee is often late because they have to drop their child off at school.
- Your employee misses deadlines because they lose time at the beginning of the day and can't work late because they must pick up their child.
- Your employee has to request personal days because they have to stay home when school is closed or when their child is sick.

Based on these issues, what **possible** and **realistic** solutions can you suggest? Remember, possible and realistic are key. But what does possible mean? Your solution has to be fair, ethical, and approved by your company.

It wouldn't be fair or ethical to tell the employee they can simply come in later and leave earlier than everyone else. And this would never be approved.

A realistic solution is one that can be easily implemented. Would it be easy to implement a plan that allowed the employee to work on Saturday to make up hours they missed during the week? No. If your company has never let anyone work weekends, there is no structure in place for this to happen.

These solutions are both possible and realistic:

- Offer the employee the opportunity to work from home when necessary.
- Offer the employee flex time so they can work outside normal business hours.

Of course, every employee would have to be given the same opportunity, so again, you would need to get this plan approved.

Develop a Plan of Action

Now that you've developed a creative and reasonable solution, you have to develop a plan of action: When and how will this all take place?

A plan of action is very similar to a set of instructions, because you must provide a numbered list of the steps that must be completed to make the solution a reality:

1. You and the employee will meet to create a flexible schedule. Two days a week the employee will work ten hours so that they can work six hours the other three days.
2. The employee will learn how to use Teams to stay in touch with the other employees when working from home.
3. The employee will meet with an HR member to formalize their new work schedule.
4. You will create a timeline for the transition.

Once you have done the work of creating a solution, you need to put your findings into a short report so that your supervisor can approve it and you can move forward.

How to Structure a Problem/Solution Document

When you write about a problem and solution, your document should include the following sections:

- Introduction
- Problem
- Solution
- Plan of Action
- Conclusion

Let's look at each of these sections more closely.

Introduction

Every document begins with an introduction, and the same is true for documents that address problems. Your introduction should state your purpose for writing, provide any necessary background information, and include a road map and a transition.

This is the same structure we looked at in the "Structure" module.

Problem

In this section, you need to do several things:

Provide any necessary background information. Remember, just because you are familiar with the causes of the problems and the people involved doesn't mean your reader is.

State the problem

When you are writing about problems and solutions, you don't want to be subtle, and you don't want to be passive-aggressive. Just state the problem:

> **Do not do this**
> If we don't address the potential issue of what could happen if overtime remains the same, I'm not sure what will happen.

This statement suggests something dire might happen, but the writer is so vague no one would be able to respond with anything other than a question. No one wants to waste time on a string of unnecessary emails, so just say what you mean.

> **Try this instead**
> If we don't cut overtime by 25 percent, we will not meet payroll next quarter.

This statement works because it quantifies the problem and states the result.

> **Do not do this**
> I am so sorry to bother you when you are busy, but I really need to talk to you about an issue that is making it difficult for me to do my job.

If the writer really cared about not wasting the reader's time, they wouldn't have sent this cryptic message.

> **Try this instead**
> I need to adjust my schedule because I no longer have a car, so I must take public transportation. The bus service from my neighborhood is unreliable, and I may no longer be able to get to work by 8:00 am.

Because this statement clearly identifies the writer's problem, the reader can consider an appropriate answer without the need for unnecessary questions.

Convince Your Reader the Problem Affects Them

If you decide to move to a new address that is farther from your workplace than your previous address, you will have to make adjustments.

However, while having to get up an hour earlier to make the longer drive is a problem for you, it is not a problem that affects your coworkers, supervisors, or company, so you can't reasonably ask to be allowed to arrive an hour late each day.

However, if someone you supervise is arriving late each day for that very reason, you do have a problem that is work related. That person's tardiness is affecting their ability to get their work done and is putting pressure on the other members of the team.

You will have to convince that person that their tardiness is a problem for both the company and them. You might explain it this way:

> We all know that commuting to the office can be difficult. It is hard to predict traffic, and public transportation isn't always reliable.
>
> However, company policy requires all of us to be in the office by 8:00, so you will have to find a way to be sure that you are no longer late. Being five or ten minutes tardy might not seem like it matters, but those five minutes add up and put pressure on your coworkers, who have to cover for you.
>
> Also, we regularly have meetings that begin at 8:00. When you are late for those meetings, you often miss valuable information that affects your work later. I want you to succeed, but until your lateness is addressed, that won't happen.

As the writer makes clear, the employee's actions not only negatively affect the team, but they also negatively affect the person and their success at their job. By demonstrating how the problem affects everyone, the writer is more likely to get cooperation from the person causing the problem. We are all the source of the problem sometime, whether we realize it or not. If we can't convince the other person that the problem is going to affect them negatively, they aren't likely to consider the problem worth solving.

Solution

Once you identify a problem, you need to offer a realistic solution that addresses the problem. This might sound simple, but it's easy to either offer a solution that doesn't address the problem or offer a solution that isn't reasonable.

Let's look at some solutions to a problem:

A valued employee didn't get a promotion because they don't have the necessary experience.

> **Do not do this**
> Offer them an extra week of vacation as a consolation.

This solution doesn't address the issue. How will an extra week of vacation give the employee the training they need? This solution isn't reasonable. Are you going to offer everyone an extra week of vacation?

> **Try this instead**
> Offer to pay for a training course so that the employee can get the training they need to be prepared for the next opportunity.

This solution addresses the issue—lack of training—and is reasonable because the company often approves training for qualified employees.

Plan of Action

A solution is only a good one if it can be made reality. Making a solution real requires a plan, and that plan must be specific. In this case, your best choice is a list of the steps that must be completed to make the solution happen. You also need to explain who is responsible for completing each step. When you tell your reader how a process will be completed, you want to use a numbered list:

1. Meet with employee to create training schedule.
2. Pay for scheduled training.
3. Meet with employee after each session for progress report.

Even though your reader might not be part of the process, they will want to be sure you have a valid plan before they approve your proposed solution.

Conclusion

Very rarely will you solve a problem without help from others, so use the conclusion to offer thanks and make it clear that you are part of the process and your door is open.

Let's look at an example. The following memo was written by an employee to their supervisor:

I am writing to you because I need your help solving a work-related issue.

As you know, for the past three years I have directed a team of six. During this period, we have gone from working in the office to working at home due to COVID, and now we are shifting back to the workplace.

Despite these many changes and challenges, my team has worked hard and well, with one exception.

Lynn.

The Problem
Lynn's productivity dropped off while we were working from home. Initially, she was completing all of her assigned reports, though typically, she submitted 10 percent of them several days late.

After we had been working at home for six months, she was no longer finishing all of her assigned reports and each of my other team members was having to add one to two of her reports to their own load. I met with her on multiple occasions to talk about strategies for staying on task, but though she responded positively to my advice when we met, her work habits did not improve. Compared to her five teammates, she finished approximately 20 percent fewer reports, and those she did finish had errors that had to be corrected by me or the other members of the team.

I had hoped her work habits would change when we were back in the office, but six weeks have passed since we returned, and her productivity has not improved.

I am hesitant to fire her because it will be very difficult to replace her, and my other team members are already overworked. I would like to give Lynn one more chance to improve. I recommend the following solution.

The Solution
Lynn has the knowledge to do her work well, as her past performance shows. However, she seems to have difficulty managing her time, and she is often off task. In order to help her with these issues, I recommend that she attend the four-week course on project management offered by the company. The course is online, so it will not interfere with her regular work schedule. I will also require her to meet with me regularly to hold her accountable. I outline my specific plan next.

Plan of Action
Over the next four weeks, I will do the following:

1. Meet with Lynn to let her know that she is on probation for the four-week period.
   At this meeting we will discuss the following:

   - Her required completion of the project management course.
   - Required meetings at 8:00 am each Monday.
   - Required meetings at 4:30 pm each Friday.
   - Requirements for continued employment: completion of course, completion of assigned tasks each week, and attendance at each meeting.
2. Meet with Lynn each Monday at 8:00 am to outline her schedule for the week.
   I will provide her with an electronic copy of her assigned duties, which she will sign.
3. Meet with Lynn each Friday at 4:30 pm to review her week's work.
   If she has completed all of her assigned tasks, I will sign off on Monday's document. If she has not, I will write her up.
4. At the end of the four weeks, I will meet with Lynn to discuss whether or not she will continue working for the company.
   During the time I have worked with you, I have been impressed by your willingness to give your employees every possible chance to succeed.

I hope that my plan will allow Lynn to do the same. If you have any questions about my proposed plan, please let me know. I would appreciate any advice you might have.

This example follows all of the best practices we have been discussing in this module. Use this as a model when doing your own writing.

But what should you do if you have a problem but you haven't been able to find a solution? Do not worry. This happens a lot.

What if I Do Not Have a Solution?

Sometimes you might face a problem you can't solve alone. In fact, your problem is that you have a problem you can't solve. In those cases, you need to ask for help. In many ways, this type of document is similar to a standard problem/solution document with one major shift. Let's look at an example:

> Hi Jake,
> Recently, several of my employees asked for my advice, and while I would like to help, I don't have an answer for them. I'm hoping you might be able to help.
>
> Three members of my team would like to learn more about project management. They took the initiative of finding a six-week course that they can take online outside of work hours. If they finish the course successfully, they will receive certificates verifying them as certified project managers. As I mentioned to you in a recent meeting, my team has been taking on many new projects, but we've been slowed down by the fact that I am the only experienced project manager on the team, which means I have to lead every project. If my three team members took the course, they would each be able to begin taking on leadership roles, which would increase our productivity as a team.
>
> While I would like to tell my team members to sign up for the course, it will cost $600 per employee. They asked me if the company could reimburse them for the cost, but I don't have the authority to make that decision. As our department manager, could you help determine if funding for this course is available?
>
> I will provide you with a course description and information about the company offering the course. Also, if you would like to meet to discuss options, I will be happy to schedule a meeting. The course begins in four weeks, so, if possible, my employees would like an answer by May 26 so they can meet the deadline to enroll.

I appreciate your help. I think this course will benefit my team members, our department, and the company. I look forward to hearing from you.

Kathryn

This email contains all the standard pieces of a problem/solution document:

Introduction
Recently, several of my employees asked for my advice, and while I would like to help, I don't have an answer for them. I'm hoping you might be able to help.

Problem
Three members of my team would like to learn more about project management. They took the initiative of finding a six-week course that they can take online outside of work hours. If they finish the course successfully, they will receive certificates verifying them as certified project managers. As I mentioned to you in a recent meeting, my team has been taking on many new projects, but we've been slowed down by the fact that I am the only experienced project manager on the team, which means I have to lead every project. If my three team members took the course, they would each be able to begin taking on leadership roles, which would increase our productivity as a team.

While I would like to tell my team members to sign up for the course, it will cost $600 per employee. They asked me if the company could reimburse them for the cost, but I don't have the authority to make that decision. As our department manager, I would like your help determining if funding for this course is available.

Solution and Plan of Action
I will provide you with a course description and information about the company offering the course. Also, if you would like to meet to discuss options, I will be happy to schedule a meeting. The course begins in four weeks, so if possible, my employees would like an answer by May 26 so they can meet the deadline to enroll.

Conclusion
I appreciate your help. I think this course will benefit my team members, our department, and the company. I look forward to hearing from you.

Assess—Problems

1. Which of the following is **NOT** a problem you would address at work?
   a. The need for a new employee
   b. The need for more office space
   c. Your need for a new car
   d. The need to update a billing process

2. Which of the following are part of the process of addressing a problem in writing?
   a. Identify the problem.
   b. Convince your readers that your problem is their problem too.
   c. Provide a solution.
   d. Develop a plan of action.
   e. All of the above

3. This is an effective statement of the problem:

   If we don't address the potential issue of what could happen if overtime remains the same, I'm not sure what will happen.
   a. True
   b. False

4. This is an effective statement of the problem:

   I need to adjust my schedule because my childcare situation has changed, and I can no longer get to work by 8:00 am because I have to drop my son off at school each morning.
   a. True
   b. False

5. Which of the following is the better solution?
   a. Offer them an extra week of vacation as a consolation.
   b. Offer to pay for a training course so that the employee can get the training they need to be prepared for the next opportunity.

Engage—Solving Problems

Problems are a regular part of work, and identifying and proposing solutions to those problems in writing is something you will be expected to do.

For this activity, your problem is an upcoming deadline that you will not be able to meet. Your task is to write to the person who can grant you an extension. In your memo, you should

- Identify the problem.
- Convince your readers that your problem is their problem.
- Provide a solution.
- Develop a plan of action.

Once your memo is complete

1. Post it to the discussion board.
2. Respond to at least three of your classmates.
3. Provide feedback on the following.
   - The content of their memo
   - The structure and design of their memo

Apply—Writing about Professional Problems

For this assignment, you must write a memo in response to the following prompt:

As with many departments, you and the members of your department have been working from home since the pandemic began. Now that business is beginning to return to normal, your company's CEO has announced that plans are being made to transition back to the workplace. To make the transition as seamless as possible, each department has been asked to submit a memo in which they address the following:

- Employee concerns
- Employee needs
- A plan for making the transition based on the following scenario:

Your supervisor has asked you to talk to each of the seven members of your department and then draft a response to the CEO.

To complete this assignment successfully, follow these steps:

1. Present your information in the form of a memo that includes the required parts of a proposal.
2. Use headings to create a visual hierarchy.
3. Follow the guidelines for creating an effective structure.
4. Use proper English grammar and spelling conventions.
5. Meet your audiences' needs.

For this assignment, you may create material concerning employee concerns and needs; however, your material must be realistic and should be based on your professional experience.

Assignment Rubric

	Superior	Above Average	Average	Below Average	Failing
Content	20 points	15 points	10 points	5 points	0 points
	Includes all of the required elements of the assignment.	Includes all of the required elements, though some are under-developed.	Includes most of the required elements.	Includes some of the required elements.	Does not include all of the required elements.

	Superior	Above Average	Average	Below Average	Failing
Style	20 points	15 points	10 points	5 points	0 points
	The writing is clear and concise and avoids unnecessary use of passive constructions.	The writing is clear and concise and generally avoids unnecessary use of passive constructions.	The writing is mostly clear and concise and mostly avoids unnecessary use of passive constructions.	The writing is occasionally clear and concise but does not avoid unnecessary use of passive constructions.	The style is inappropriate or unclear.
Design	20 points	15 points	10 points	5 points	0 points
	The document has a clear visual hierarchy and the writer uses appropriate methods of presentation such as lists and tables.	The document has a clear visual hierarchy and the writer uses some appropriate methods of presentation such as lists and tables.	The document has a basic visual hierarchy and the writer occasionally uses appropriate methods of presentation such as lists and tables.	The document's visual hierarchy is weak and the writer doesn't use appropriate methods of presentation such as lists and tables.	The document has no visual hierarchy.
Structure	20 points	15 points	10 points	5 points	0 points
	The organization of the document is clear and logical and makes strong use of topic sentences and transitions.	The organization of the document is generally clear and logical and makes some use of topic sentences and transitions.	The document has an organization and occasionally uses topic sentences and transitions.	The structure is weak and the writer rarely uses topic sentences or transitions.	The document has no structure.
Correctness	20 points	15 points	10 points	5 points	0 points
	The document has no errors.	The document has 2–3 errors.	The document has 4–5 errors.	The document has 6–7 errors.	The document has 8 or more errors.

Sharing

Learning Objectives
- Recognize the types of informational documents.
- Understand when to share information.
- Respond to a request for information.
- Structure an informational document.
- Write short informational documents.
- Write long informational documents.

Learn—Sharing Information

We don't write professional documents just for the fun of it. We write for a specific reason, and one of the keys to writing effectively is knowing why we write. One common reason for writing is to share information. If I had to guess, I'd say at least 90 percent of the emails that I write have the goal of sharing information. Sometimes, as in this example, I was asked for specific information. Sometimes, I anticipate a question and provide information before I am asked.

Let's take a look at an example email to see this in action.

Statement of Purpose	Hi, how are you? I got your email asking for more information about the course I've been developing, UCRS: Professional Development. Below, I've included the course description:
Requested Information	Students will learn to translate their academic skills into marketable skills as they seek to make their professional goals a reality. The skills acquired will prepare students to apply for internships, jobs, grants, business loans, and postgraduate educational opportunities.

153

	Students will practice different methods of articulating how their academic skills qualify them for professional opportunities. Some of the methods of communication practiced will include writing professional emails, reports, and job materials; interviewing; working as an effective member of a team; becoming an effective leader; giving professional presentations; practicing diverse and inclusive methods of professionalism; and becoming digitally literate.
	Students will engage in professional activities such as mock interviews, professional mixers, and conferences to develop the social skills they need to succeed in the professional world. Students will complete the course by preparing to apply for an internship, job, loan, or other professional option (to be approved by the instructor).
	This professional proposal will ensure that students leave the course with a written plan of action for achieving their career goals upon graduation and becoming forces of positive change.
Offered additional information	I hope the description was helpful, but should you need more detail, I've attached the course syllabus.
Open line of communication	Please let me know if you have any more questions.

As you see from the example, I did several specific things in this email:

- Restated the request for information I received
- Identified the first piece of information I provided
- Identified additional information I provided
- Made it clear that I was willing to answer questions

I was able to know what to include because I considered my audience and their request first.

Consider Your Audience

When we write to share information, we are providing specific information for a specific purpose. So we have to decide what information our audience needs—and this means taking care to remember that we know more than our audience, so their needs determine what we include. Finally, we have to provide enough detail to meet their needs.

Writing to share information is much like writing to respond, which we'll discuss later; however, there is one major difference:

- When we write to respond, the **writer** decides what information is being shared and why.
- When we write to provide information, the **reader** (who made the original request for information) determines what information is shared and why.

An answer to a response for information can come in many forms:

- You will send emails that answer questions.
- You will send text messages that include times and dates for meetings.
- You will provide data that will be used in reports.

These are just a few examples of the types of documents you might write to share information. We can't possibly predict them all.

Why Should You Learn How to Share Information Effectively?

Before we go any further, let's get this out of the way. The importance of sharing information effectively isn't a concept we invented just for this book. Working professionals have a lot to say about this subject:

> Poor communication in the business environment can be very costly. It could lead to decisions that are made using false assumptions and unreliable data. Such problems can cost organizations an average of more than $7,000 a day. There are various reasons why wrong information can be creeping into your organization right now: unclear instructions and expectations, poor listening skills, unreliable data, lack of collaboration among team members and the list goes on. One of the leading communication issues involves teams and departments operating in silos and not sharing information.

> This lack of collaboration can kill a growing business. So can this be solved? Here's an idea: Promote a single version of truth in your business. By this, I mean that your business should espouse transparency and better sharing of data and information across the organization. This can be done with the help of cloud-based solutions that promote transparency and collaboration. (Johnson 2020)

Here's another opinion:

> If you've ever experienced a long email chain wherein respondents ask multiple questions to clarify the original email, you'll understand the importance of efficient communication. Having sharply honed writing skills can help you clearly and quickly communicate updates, events, projects, or other important topics to co-workers without requiring additional time for clarification or questions. (Tulane University School of Professional Advancement 2023)

Whether you are writing a short email or a longer report, every document that shares information uses the same basic structure.

How to Structure an Informational Document

When providing information, you first must decide whether to take the direct or indirect approach. Each approach has its own unique advantages, disadvantages, and appropriate uses. Deciding which approach you are going to use in your document is incredibly important and determines the appropriate structure.

When Is a Direct Approach the Best Choice?

When you are providing information your readers will likely be happy to get, use a direct approach:

- Here are the details about our holiday party.
- Everyone is getting a 5 percent cost-of-living raise.

When Is an Indirect Approach Best?
If you are giving information that your reader may not like, use an indirect approach:

- The company is instituting a new dress code.
- Gym memberships are being canceled.
- We cannot make a new hire.

Let's look at how to structure both a direct and indirect request.

Using a Direct Approach
When you write to share information using a direct approach, use this structure:

Introduction
Why you are sharing information

Body
Detailed information about the new policy or procedure

Conclusion
Includes a call to action and demonstrates that the lines of communication are still open

Each of the pieces of the structure serves a specific purpose.

Introduction
Anytime we communicate with someone for a professional reason, we should begin by stating our purpose.
Why?
Because everyone is busy, and if you can't convince someone from the first line that a communication is important to them, they probably won't read it. This might sound harsh, but your readers need to know what's in it for them. Think of how many texts, emails, and tweets you are bombarded with every day. The only way to keep up is by prioritizing, and we prioritize based on choosing those communications that offer us something we need. So every time you write to share information, your introduction should include

- A statement of purpose
- What information you are providing
- What's in it for your reader

Let's look at some examples of some openings for an email:

Email Opening Examples

> Next week the company will be implementing a new policy.

Good or Bad?

This example doesn't work because it doesn't tell the reader much at all:

- Why is the company implementing a new policy?
- What is the policy?
- Does the new policy affect the reader?

> In this email, I provide an overview of our new procedure for requesting time off. Because the old procedure caused employees' requests for time off to be delayed, beginning July 1, you should follow the procedure I outline below when you ask for time off. Employees who do not use the new procedure will not have their requests processed.

Good or Bad?

This second example is much better because it makes it clear what procedure is being changed, why, and how the change will benefit the readers. This is an excellent opening.

After your statement of purpose, you need to provide details about the information you are providing.

Body

If you don't provide accurate, specific information, how can you expect your reader to comply? For example, if you schedule a meeting and provide the wrong time, who is at fault if no one attends? The portion of your message in which you provide details might be one or more paragraphs long. The length will be based on the amount and complexity of the information. But you need to remember these rules:

Rule	Example
Be specific	If you give a time, give an exact time: July 16 at 8:00 am.
Be accurate	If a new procedure is required rather than suggested, make that clear. Otherwise, you, not you readers, are to blame if someone chooses not to follow the procedure.
Be complete	If a procedure has multiple steps, include all of them.

Once you have provided all of the information, be sure to tell your reader what to do with it.

Conclusion

The final paragraph of our message must do two things:

- Provide a statement of action.
- Show that the lines of communication are open.

Provide a Statement of Action

Most of us have a profile on LinkedIn. The purpose of your profile is to share information about yourself with other professionals. However, if your summary doesn't end with a call to action, your readers won't know how to respond. What to do you need from your readers? Advice, a job, an internship? If you don't tell them, they won't provide it. Here are some good action statements:

- If you have any information regarding internships in accounting in the Dallas area, please contact me.
- If you have any questions regarding the new procedure for requesting time off, please send me an email. Human Resources is also hosting a lunch meeting on Wednesday, August 3, at noon.

Finally, you need to keep the conversation going.

Show That the Lines of Communication Are Open

Your readers need to know that you are available to answer questions, or that other sources of clarification are available. Otherwise, readers may not understand the information you shared, and if they have no one to go to with questions, they may unintentionally make mistakes.

Using an Indirect Approach

When you provide unwanted information, you must be sure the reader understands why what you are sharing is necessary and how it will benefit them.

Introduction
Rather than bluntly sharing your information, you should begin with a buffer that emphasizes the positive by showing appreciation.

Body
Show empathy and provide a justification for the request to come. Tell employees how complying with the request will benefit them. Include a call to action.

Conclusion
Keep the communication open and provide opportunities for clarification or questions.

Let's take a look at this structure in action:

Function	Example
Introduction	Our department is very successful, and our success is largely due to your individual levels of professionalism. However, the company knows you are capable of even more, so they are beginning a new Dress for Success initiative.
Body with specific detail	Customers judge our level of professionalism based on first appearances, and we want our first impression to be a strong one. To help us reach this goal, starting on September 1, we will all follow the new Dress for Success guidelines:
	Monday–Thursday: Business casual (slacks, collared shirts, dresses, skirts, etc.) **Friday**: Company spirit (company-branded shirts, slacks, jeans, dressy sneakers, etc.)
	A more complete list will be emailed to each of you next week.

Function	Example
Body with specific detail	Don't worry. No one expects you to buy a new wardrobe. Local department stores are offering us employee discounts of 25 percent. You will receive instructions for getting your discount via email. Also, the company has a lending closet. You can borrow work-appropriate attire for free. However, you will need to have the clothing you borrow dry-cleaned before you return it.
Conclusion	I appreciate all you do for the company, and I know that this new initiative will make us even better than we already are. An information session is being held July 27 at noon. Lunch will be provided, and you can ask questions. I hope to see you there. And as always, my door is open if you have questions or concerns about being ready on September 1.

Now that you understand how to structure a message that shares information, let's look at some best practices that will help you make good decisions as you write.

- Understand what information is needed.
- Make sure your information is accurate.
- Make sure your information is complete.
- Make sure you keep a record of the information.
- Make sure you send it to everyone who needs it.

Let's look at each of these more carefully.

Understand What Information Is Needed

Before you begin to write, you need to carefully consider what to include in your message. Here are some questions to answer that will help you decide:

- What do your readers already know about the information you are sharing? Have they been part of the decision-making process? Are they hearing about this topic for the first time?
- What questions are they likely to have? Will they want to know when something will happen? Where? Why? How?
- What is your readers' attitude likely to be? Will they be pleased with the information, or worried, indecisive, or resistant?

- What do you want them to do with the information you provide? Do you want them to cooperate? Act, understand, participate?

The best way to be sure if you have provided the information your readers need is to ask someone who is in your audience!

NOTE	Do you know how many times this book was proofread before it was published? Writers often have multiple colleagues review their writing in addition to their own reviews. Even professional writers need their work reviewed by others, so never be afraid to ask someone else to review yours.

Make Sure Your Information Is Accurate

If your information isn't accurate, it's useless, and any problems that occur because of your error will be your fault. For example, if you send your team an email telling them you have scheduled a meeting for the fourteenth when you meant the fifteenth, you have no reason to be mad at your team when they don't come to the meeting on the fourteenth. Or what if you meant to attach the document dated 3/13 but instead you accidentally attached an earlier version of the same document? Here are some strategies for checking the accuracy of your information:

Slow down	It's easy to get busy and neglect to proofread your own work. This is a fatal error. Proofreading your work is not something you do when you have the time. It's something you do every time! Make this a habit.
Ask	Don't assume; no one knows everything. If you don't know something, or you aren't 100 percent sure, ask the person who has the answer. This isn't a waste of your time or theirs because everyone will benefit.

Make Sure Your Information Is Complete

When you are sharing information with others, it is usually because you are an expert. In other words, you know more than everyone else. When we know more than others, it is easy to fall into the trap of forgetting our readers don't know as much as we do. When we think that way, we can easily leave out information our readers need:

- Definitions of terms
- A summary of previous work or decisions
- Deadlines
- Work delegation

It is better to risk repeating something your readers already know rather than leaving out something they need.

Make Sure You Keep a Record of the Information

We aren't suggesting that you keep every email you write in your inbox. However, you should create electronic folders to keep copies of important information. We suggest using a resource like Dropbox or Teams. Why do you need to keep digital records?

Sometimes someone might question whether you actually sent a particular piece of information. If you have kept a copy of that communication, you can easily answer the question. Or you or someone you work with might not remember a particular detail from a previous document. Again, if you have saved the document, you can quickly find the answer.

Make Sure You Send It to Everyone Who Needs It

Sending out electronic documents has its issues. It's easy to attach a document to an existing email without checking who's on the mailing list. Ouch.

You just sent your document to three people who don't need it. Now you have to answer their annoyed, confused questions.

> **TIP**
>
> Rather than relying on existing messages, begin a new message every time you send or attach a document. This simple practice can help you ensure you only give information to those who want, need, and expect it.

Assess—Writing to Share Information

1. Which of the following should a statement of purpose include?
   a. Identify what information you are providing.
   b. Begin with a demand.
   c. Ignore the readers' needs. You are the leader.
   d. Tell your reader what's in it for them.

2. Which statement does NOT describe the necessary qualities of detailed information?
   a. Short. You can talk to everyone at lunch.
   b. Accurate
   c. Specific
   d. Complete

3. Which of the following should the closing include? Select all that apply.
   a. Include as little as possible.
   b. Provide a statement of action.
   c. Show the lines of communication are open.
   d. A closing is optional.

4. Which of the following is NOT a good reason for showing your readers the lines of communication are open?
   a. So your readers know they can ask questions
   b. So you can correct any misunderstandings
   c. So you can create goodwill
   d. So you can criticize the people who come in

5. Which of the following are not good reasons for sharing information? Check all that apply.
   a. To let everyone know about upcoming changes
   b. To share photos of your amazing vacation
   c. To provide details about an upcoming project
   d. To answer questions

Engage—Writing to Share Information

Recently, your department has been facing an issue. When your company first opened, it was small and family owned and operated. While the size of the company has tripled, the policies and procedures that the company follows have not kept up. As a consequence, employees have been taking personal days and half days without prior approval, which is causing scheduling issues and other problems. In order to improve the situation, the company is formalizing its procedures for taking time off. The following memo was written by your supervisor, who asked you to give your feedback before they send it out.

Memo

Date: April 29, 2022
To: Members of the Human Resources Department
From: Jo Manager
Re: It's time to stop

When all the employees at this company were members of the same family, it was okay for people to just take time off without thinking about anyone else. But now all kinds of people work here, but you all still act like we're one big family. You have to stop randomly taking time off! Just last week, I had to work on Saturday to cover for someone who did not let me know until Friday that they had to miss their shift to go to a wedding! I had plans too, but I had to cancel them. And don't get me started on the women with kids!

I'm not the only one who has a problem with your behavior. The CEO of the company has issued a new policy that everyone has to follow. Everyone! I have summarized the policy below.

Starting next month, we will follow this procedure for requesting time off. All requests for time off must be made at least six weeks in advance. No exceptions. Requests have to be made in writing using the appropriate online form. All requests must be approved.

I don't mean to be harsh, but you have to clean up your acts.

To complete this activity successfully, complete the following steps:

1. Determine whether the writer achieved the following:
   - Used an appropriate tone for the audience.
   - Used an indirect approach.
   - Included adequate and accurate information.
   - Ended with a call to action.
   - Showed the conversation was open.
   - Crafted a memo with an effective structure.
   - Wrote the memo with no errors in style, grammar, or punctuation.
2. After assessing the above, complete the following:
   a. Present your findings in a memo.
   b. Post your memo to the discussion.
   c. Respond to at least three of your classmates. Provide feedback on the following:
      - The content of their memo
      - The structure and design of their memo

Apply—Sharing information

For this assignment, you must write a memo in response to the following prompt:

In the "Audience" module you identified the problems facing the members of your department as the company transitions from work at home to work from the office. After identifying the problems, you suggested a potential solution based on what you learned from interviewing the members of your department. Now that your proposed plan and solution has been approved by the CEO, your job is to share it with the members of your department.

Most of the department has enjoyed the convenience of working from home and have concerns about returning to the office. Your job is to present the information as persuasively as possible to get everyone's cooperation.

To complete this assignment successfully, follow these steps:

1. Present your information in the form of a memo.
2. Use headings to create a visual hierarchy.

3. Follow the guidelines for creating an effective structure.
4. Use correct English.
5. Meet your audiences' needs.

For this assignment, you may create material concerning employee concerns and needs; however, your material must be realistic and should be based on your professional experience.

Assignment Rubric

	Superior	Above Average	Average	Below Average	Failing
Content	20 points	15 points	10 points	5 points	0 points
	Includes all of the required elements of the assignment.	Includes all of the required elements, though some are under-developed.	Includes most of the required elements.	Includes some of the required elements.	Does not include all of the required elements.
Style	20 points	15 points	10 points	5 points	0 points
	The writing is clear and concise and avoids unnecessary use of passive constructions.	The writing is clear and concise and generally avoids unnecessary use of passive constructions.	The writing is mostly clear and concise and mostly avoids unnecessary use of passive constructions.	The writing is occasionally clear and concise but does not avoid unnecessary use of passive constructions.	The style is inappropriate or unclear.
Design	20 points	15 points	10 points	5 points	0 points
	The document has a clear visual hierarchy and the writer uses appropriate methods of presentation such as lists and tables.	The document has a clear visual hierarchy and the writer uses some appropriate methods of presentation such as lists and tables.	The document has a basic visual hierarchy and the writer occasionally uses appropriate methods of presentation such as lists and tables.	The document's visual hierarchy is weak and the writer doesn't use appropriate methods of presentation such as lists and tables.	The document has no visual hierarchy.

	Superior	*Above Average*	*Average*	*Below Average*	*Failing*
Structure	20 points	15 points	10 points	5 points	0 points
	The organization of the document is clear and logical and makes strong use of topic sentences and transitions.	The organization of the document is generally clear and logical and makes some use of topic sentences and transitions.	The document has an organization and occasionally uses topic sentences and transitions.	The structure is weak and the writer rarely uses topic sentences or transitions.	The document has no structure.
Correctness	20 points	15 points	10 points	5 points	0 points
	The document has no errors.	The document has 2–3 errors.	The document has 4–5 errors.	The document has 6–7 errors.	The document has 8 or more errors.

Make and Respond to Requests

Learning Objectives
- Recognize written requests.
- Understand when to make a request.
- Respond to a request.
- Structure a request.
- Write a short request.
- Write a longer request.

Learn—Requests

Writing to Make Requests

In the previous module, you learned how to provide information. But what if you need information from someone else? Your best method for getting it is to request it.

Ask for What You Need

Asking for what we need seems like a simple process. For example, maybe you ask your team leader to take you off of the next day's meeting agenda because you need more time to finish your report. Next week would be better. You know your team leader is reasonable, so you make your request when you happen to run into her at the coffee machine: "I'm still running the data. Could I give my presentation at next week's meeting?" She gives you a distracted smile and says, "Sure. No problem." You can tell she's busy, so you smile and let her get back to work.

The next day at the meeting, you are listening to your team-mates' progress reports and considering what you will say during next week's meeting. Suddenly, your team leader looks at you and says, "Okay. Your turn. Let's hear your report on your data analysis." Ten pairs of eyes are looking at you. In a panic, you look at your team lead and blurt out, "You told me yesterday that I didn't have to give my report! Did you forget?"

After a quick glance at you, she calls on the next person. For the next hour, you are so busy feeling mistreated that you can hardly pay attention. When the meeting ends, the team lead quietly asks you to stay behind for a minute. "Good," you think. "She's going to apologize to me."

To your surprise, the conversation takes a very different turn:

Team Lead:	Could you please tell me why you didn't have your report ready? Your analysis is a crucial part of keeping this project on time.
You:	I asked you to move me to next week's meeting yesterday, and you said okay.
Team Lead:	When yesterday? I don't recall getting your email.
You:	I didn't send an email. I asked you when you were getting coffee.
Team Lead:	(After sighing heavily) I'm sure you did ask, and perhaps I should have paid more attention, but I don't expect my team members to make important requests while I'm getting coffee.
	If I had had time to think about your request, I would have said no because an incomplete report would have been more useful than no report. But let's consider this a learning experience.
	When you are making a request that affects not just you but your entire team, put it in writing so that the person you are asking has time to consider the implications of your request.
You:	I didn't want to bother you with another email!
Team Lead:	A written request that can affect our team's project isn't a bother. What's a bother is the situation we are in now. From now on put important requests in writing.

Although this scenario may be fictional, it addresses a very important mistake that many professionals make: not providing a written record of important requests. It is crucial to ALWAYS put important requests in writing.

But what types of requests should we consider important?

When to Put a Request in Writing

When deciding whether to put a request in writing, ask yourself these questions:

- Does this request affect anyone other than me?
- If the answer to my request is no, will I be prepared for the consequences?
- Do I need a record of my request and my answer?

Let's consider some different scenarios:

You, to your colleague in the next cubicle:	I'm running to the coffee shop. Want anything?

This request does not need to be in writing. If doesn't affect your work, and whether they say yes or no will not affect anyone other than you.

You, to another member of your team:	I was supposed to pick up breakfast at Eli's tomorrow before our meeting. Could you do it instead? I need time to finish my report.

This request needs to be in writing. First, you shouldn't expect your coworker to answer you on the spot; that isn't fair. Second, if they say yes, you need a record of that response in case something goes wrong. Finally, if they say no, you need a reminder to make another plan because the whole team will be affected if breakfast doesn't arrive. Ultimately, you were responsible for picking it up, and the blame will go to you.

These requests are fairly simple, but the more complex the request, the more important it is for the request to be in writing and the longer your document is likely to be. But short or long, all written requests follow a standard format.

Structuring a Written Request

As we learned in "Writing to Share Information," first you need to decide whether to take a direct or indirect approach.

When Is a Direct Approach the Best Choice?

When you make a request that your readers will likely be happy to grant, use a direct approach:

- Would you accept a promotion?
- Would you like to watch the hockey game Saturday from the company's luxury box?

When Is an Indirect Approach Best?

If you are making a request that your reader may not like, use an indirect approach:

- Can you work on Saturday?
- John is out sick. Could you write his portion of the report that is due Monday? He hasn't started yet.
- Could the company reimburse me for $950 to cover the cost of a course I took on programming in Python?

Let's look at how to structure both a direct and indirect request.

How to Structure a Direct Request

When you make a direct request, you get right to the point, but that doesn't mean you don't need to begin with an introduction. Whether you are making a short request in an email or attaching a longer document, a direct request uses this structure:

1. Introduction: statement of purpose (request)
2. Body: detail about the request being made
3. Conclusion: call to action

Now let's look at an example.

Request	I have been asked to choose someone to attend the marketing conference in New York City, and I would like you to go.
Body	The conference begins on October 11 and ends on the 13th. I have made reservations at the conference hotel: The Wyndham New Yorker in Manhattan. If you decide to go, you can arrange your flight with Michael in Human Resources. All of your meals are included as part of the conference registration fee, and you will be reimbursed for any meals you have at the airport, but remember to keep your receipts.

Conclusion	If you decide to go to the conference, please respond to this email by Monday at 5:00 so I have time to offer the trip to someone else if you can't go. Feel free to contact me if you have any questions.

Some requests are harder to make because we know the person who is receiving the request may not want to do what we've asked. These types of situations require a slightly different structure.

How to Structure an Indirect Request

When you ask someone to do something that they might not want to do, you have to find a way to persuade them not just to cooperate but to do it willingly.

When I explained this to one of my students, they said, "I don't know why you can't just tell them to do it. Work is work. If you want to keep your job, you do what you're told."

To some degree this is true. On the other hand, consider this:

- Employees can find other jobs.
- Employees who feel they have been treated unfairly can create a negative work environment.
- Doesn't every employee deserve to understand why a request was made and why they should comply?

Because all of these points are true, we need to address them in the structure of an indirect written request.

Introduction
Rather than bluntly making your request, you should begin with a buffer that emphasizes the positive by showing appreciation.

Body
Show empathy. Provide a justification for the request to come. Tell employees how complying with the request will benefit them.

Conclusion
Acknowledge any inconveniences and leave the door open for questions.

Let's look at an example.

Introduction	Another quarter has ended successfully. Despite the effects of COVID, our company remains open. Our success is due to the hard work of each employee. We couldn't do it without you.
Body	We survived the quarter, but if we are going to survive the next, we will have to make some difficult changes. The directors of each division have been asked to reduce their budgets by 10 percent. I have considered how to meet this goal, and I have determined that we have two choices. I can let a member of our team go, or we can each voluntarily take a 10 percent pay cut until business improves. I don't want to make this decision alone, so I am asking each of you to agree to the pay cut.
	I understand that I am asking a lot. Our company relies largely on the hospitality industry for our business, and because of COVID, most restaurants and bars have been closed. This situation is already improving, as is our business, but the budget reduction is necessary to get us through this lean time.
	No one wants to take a pay cut, but a temporary pay cut is much better than losing your job. Also, if we lose a team member, the workload of those of us who remain will increase. If we all take the pay cut, our workload will not be affected. Also, your cooperation will help protect each of your jobs for the future by lessening the company's financial risk. You will begin receiving your full salary once the economy recovers.
	Please respond to this email and let me know if you will accept the pay cut or if you prefer me to eliminate someone's position. If I don't get complete agreement regarding the pay cuts, I will not make them.
Conclusion	I realize this is a sensitive issue, so please take the rest of this week to consider your decision. I am available to answer your questions if you have any.

Now that you understand how to structure a request, let's look at some basic principles that will help you make good decisions as you write:

- Be sure your request is reasonable.
- Provide compelling support.
- Do your homework.
- Lose gracefully.
- Don't throw others under the bus.

Let's look at each of these more closely.

Be Sure Your Request Is Reasonable

It's important to have the confidence to ask for what you need professionally, but you can't just consider your own needs. You also have to consider the needs of your department and company because, ultimately, they will approve or disapprove your request based on whether they think it will benefit them as well as you. Consider this scenario:

> You plan to ask your supervisor to reimburse you for the cost of taking a course.
>
> Which course do you think would be approved?
>
> • Advanced Project Management Strategies
>
> • Introduction to Creative Writing

Because you work as a project manager, you can easily argue that taking the course in Advanced Project Management Strategies would benefit both you and the company by making you better at your job. This request would likely be approved.

On the other hand, while you are an aspiring writer, your skills as a novelist will not benefit your company. This request would be denied.

Provide Compelling Support

When you make a request, small or large, the person you are asking needs information in order to make an informed decision. If you don't provide the information, your request will probably be denied—not because your supervisor is unfair, but because you didn't give them enough information to justify saying yes.

For example, if you did want to request to be reimbursed for the cost of taking a course that would help you do your job better, you need to tell your supervisor:

- What the course will teach you
- How that knowledge will directly benefit the company
- The cost of the course
- Whether you will miss any time at work, and if so, how you will make it up

Do Your Homework

The best way to provide compelling support is to do your homework.

Don't ask to be reimbursed without first finding out exactly how much you are asking for. Don't obligate a colleague to do anything without first talking to that person and getting their written approval.

Even if you are asking for something as simple as having a new ink cartridge ordered for your printer, be sure you know the model number before you ask.

Lose Gracefully

Even if you do your homework and provide compelling reasons to approve your request, sometimes the answer will still be no. In those situations, find out what you can regarding the decision so you understand and can be prepared in the future, then let it go.

Don't Throw Others under the Bus

When you ask someone you work with to grant a work-related request, you automatically put that person at some risk because whether they say yes or no to your request, you have involved them.

Don't ask a colleague to do something that puts them in jeopardy. For example, asking a colleague to cover for you while you make a phone call might seem like nothing. But what if your supervisor needs you while you are gone and your colleague lies to protect you? Now your colleague could get in trouble as well as you.

If you ask a colleague to help you with a project, or to do a job you were asked to do, give that person credit for the work they did, and get your supervisor's approval before you make the request.

Take responsibility for your own actions!

Assess—Requests

1. Why should you make a professional request in writing? Choose the best answer.
   a. To ensure that you include all the pertinent details so your reader can respond with what you need
   b. You shouldn't; just ask someone directly
   c. Because you want them to know you are more important than they are
   d. Because it will impress your supervisor

2. Which statement does NOT give a good reason for making a request in writing?
   a. This request affects my whole team.
   b. If the answer to my request is no, I might not be prepared.
   c. I want to ask my supervisor if she wants to come to my wedding.
   d. I need a record of my request and the answer I receive.

3. Which of the following should the closing include? Select all that apply.
   a. Include as little as possible.
   b. Provide a statement of action.
   c. Show the lines of communication are open.
   d. A closing is optional.

4. Which of the following statements is NOT a good reason for showing your readers the lines of communication are open?
   a. So your readers know they can ask questions
   b. So you can correct any misunderstandings
   c. So you can create goodwill
   d. So you can criticize the people who come in

5. Which of the following are not good reasons for sharing information? Check all that apply.
   a. To let everyone know about upcoming changes
   b. To share photos of your amazing vacation
   c. To provide details about an upcoming project
   d. To answer questions

Engage—Requests

Discussion Activity

For this activity, you will write a memo in which you request your supervisor to reimburse you for the cost of this course. However, before you can put your request in writing, you need to determine whether to use a direct or indirect approach. Once you decide, you can choose the appropriate structure for your memo. Once your memo is complete,

1. Post it to the discussion board.
2. Respond to three other posts.
3. Respond to at
4. List three of your classmates.
5. Provide feedback on the following:
   a. The appropriateness of the approach
   b. The content of their memo
   c. The structure and design of their memo

Apply—Requests

For this assignment, you must write a memo in response to the following prompt:

You have just learned that your department will no longer be working from home as you have for the past eight months. Although the transition period from home to office is four weeks, you do not feel prepared to return to the office that quickly. Although you addressed your concerns when your colleague interviewed you when preparing a proposal for the CEO, in order to get permission to be exempted from the proposed plan, you must put your request in writing for your supervisor to approve.

Based on your situation, write a memo asking your supervisor to allow you to continue working from home for a specified period of time.

To complete this assignment successfully, follow these steps:

- Present your information in the form of a memo.
- Use headings to create a visual hierarchy.

- Follow the guidelines for creating an effective structure.
- Use correct English.
- Meet your audiences' needs.

For this assignment, you may create material concerning employee concerns and needs; however, your material must be realistic and should be based on your professional experience.

Assignment Rubric

	Superior	Above Average	Average	Below Average	Failing
Content	20 points	15 points	10 points	5 points	0 points
	Includes all of the required elements of the assignment.	Includes all of the required elements, though some are under-developed.	Includes most of the required elements.	Includes some of the required elements.	Does not include all of the required elements.
Style	20 points	15 points	10 points	5 points	0 points
	The writing is clear and concise and avoids unnecessary use of passive con-structions.	The writing is clear and concise and generally avoids unnecessary use of passive constructions.	The writing is mostly clear and concise and mostly avoids unnecessary use of passive con-structions.	The writing is occasionally clear and concise but does not avoid unnecessary use of passive con-structions.	The style is inappropriate or unclear.
Design	20 points	15 points	10 points	5 points	0 points
	The document has a clear visual hierarchy and the writer uses appropriate methods of presentation such as lists and tables.	The document has a clear visual hierarchy and the writer uses some appropriate methods of presentation such as lists and tables.	The document has a basic visual hierarchy and the writer occasionally uses appropriate methods of presentation such as lists and tables.	The document's visual hierarchy is weak and the writer doesn't use appropriate methods of presentation such as lists and tables.	The document has no visual hierarchy.

	Superior	*Above Average*	*Average*	*Below Average*	*Failing*
Structure	20 points	15 points	10 points	5 points	0 points
	The organization of the document is clear and logical and makes strong use of topic sentences and transitions.	The organization of the document is generally clear and logical and makes some use of topic sentences and transitions.	The document has an organization and occasionally uses topic sentences and transitions.	The structure is weak and the writer rarely uses topic sentences or transitions.	The document has no structure.
Correctness	20 points	15 points	10 points	5 points	0 points
	The document has no errors.	The document has 2–3 errors.	The document has 4–5 errors.	The document has 6–7 errors.	The document has 8 or more errors.

Bibliography

Carroll, L. (1869). *Alice's Adventures in Wonderland*. London: Macmillan.

Herrity, J. (2023, March 16). "How to Write a Professional Email (With Tips and Examples)." Indeed.com. https://www.indeed.com/career-advice/career-development/how-to-write-a-professional-email.

Johnson, W. (2020, January 22). "4 Benefits of Sharing Information in the Workplace." Small Business Trends. https://smallbiztrends.com/2017/01/benefits-of-sharing-information-in-the-workplace.html.

Moore, K. (2016, April 7). "Study: 73% of Employers Want Candidates with This Skill." Inc. https://www.inc.com/kaleigh-moore/study-73-of-employers-want-candidates-with-this-skill.html.

Tulane University School of Professional Advancement. (2023, April 12). "The Importance of Writing Skills in the Workplace." https://sopa.tulane.edu/blog/importance-writing-skills-workplace.

Updike, J. (1981). *Rabbit Run*. New York: Alfred A. Knopf.

Index

Printed in the USA
CPSIA information can be obtained
at www.ICGtesting.com
JSHW021101270823
47091JS00003B/4